Joan!
Thank you for
inspiring our
Students
Pat Hagan

Congrats!
Joan!
Chef Johnny G.

Nicole
Kim

Many Thanks Joan!
All the best - Matt

BRAVO JOAN!

We are so appreciative
of your continued
support...
Chef K. B. 2015

Thanks!
- Bittany
Murkney

Congrats Joan

Best Wishes
from another
Disciples
Chef Michael Scott

Congrats Joan

Thank you so very much
Vivienne

Joan, giving Joan
Simply giving

Thank you so much for
inspiring everyone.
Chef Brant

A Culinary Legacy
From Escoffier to Today

Karen Blumensaadt-Stoeckley & Max Callegari

Photography by Curt Dennison

Courtesy and copyright of Jacqui Brown from www.frenchvillagediaries.com.

Acclaim Press
TM
— Your Next Great Book —

P.O. Box 238
Morley, MO 63767
(573) 472-9800
www.acclaimpress.com

Cover Photography: Curt Dennison
Cover Design: M. Frene Melton
Book Layout: M. Frene Melton

ISBN-10: 1-938905-42-3
ISBN-13: 978-1-938905-42-1
Library of Congress Control Number: 2013954907

First Printing: 2014
Printed in the United States of America
10 9 8 7 6 5 4 3 2 1

This publication was produced using available information.
The publisher regrets it cannot assume responsibility for errors or omissions.

Contents

Foreword

By Michel A. Escoffier

About Auguste Escoffier (1846-1935)

I met Karen in the south of France when she visited the Escoffier Foundation and Museum of Culinary Art, and she shared with me her project to revive her grandfather's work that she thought was somewhat inspired by my great-grandfather. When young Axel decided, at the age of 16, to move from his native homeland to Paris to learn the trade of cook, Auguste Escoffier was at the summit of his reputation in London and just about to leave the Savoy Hotel with his partner Cesar Ritz to open the Ritz Hotel in Paris.

A year later, in 1899, both men went back to London to open the Carlton Hotel, where Escoffier continued to delight the world until 1920. Those were the most prolific years of his long and fruitful career. He created a mutual assistance fund for cooks and introduced the first fund-raising dinners to finance it, continued his daily arrangement with the Little Sisters of the Poor that he had started at the Savoy, whereby he provided them with unserved food from the day before and recipes to prepare it, served as a consultant to the Hamburg Amerika Line to create the Ritz-Carlton restaurants, co-founded Westminster College culinary department, and yet found time to write an essay on the extinction of poverty (a social scourge), launch a magazine – *Le Carnet d'Epicure* – and above all, publish *Le Guide Culinaire*, followed a few years later by *Le Livre des Menus*. No wonder he was regarded, already in his lifetime, as the greatest culinary artist of modern times.

The basic principles of cooking and organizational methods layed out by Auguste Escoffier have been applied and followed the world over and are still very much in practice today. Very few men in history have as deeply influenced their profession as he did, not only through time and his exemplary work, but also through the significant changes and innovations he introduced and the teaching techniques he passed on to future generations. Indeed, he was quite a visionary, when he writes in the introduction of his Guide Culinaire, first published over a century ago, that "cooking, like fashion, has to evolve with time and we need to take into account the fundamental changes that will inevitably occur in people's lives, which are constantly accelerating. We will therefore gradually introduce lighter dishes and shorter menus." In the Livre des

Michel A. Escoffier

Menus that followed he adds: "cooking, whilst remaining an art, will become more scientific and precise, but at the same time we will enhance the nutritive and taste values of dishes."

Auguste strived all his life to improve the status of the chef and bring esteem for his profession. He introduced behavioral standards and greatly improved the working conditions in the kitchen.

He was an apostle and as such, felt that he had to convey his message to disciples who would hand it on to the generations to come. He was mostly proud of having trained over 2,000 chefs who subsequently went on to promote French culinary art around the world. He always insisted that the primary aim of a cook must be perfection, for it's own sake, and to never be satisfied with anything but the best. And that implied simplicity and honesty. As an example, sauces should not camouflage the main ingredient but enhance it. He also never ceased to advocate the importance of quality, as much for the product as for the realization. He disliked intensely all complicated recipes as well as incomprehensible titles for them, and loathed every form of sham and make-believe in the kitchen, or anywhere else for that matter. He often deplored the crazy search for novelty at all costs, although he introduced more innovations than most chefs ever did before him or since.

Today, often referred to as "King of Chefs and Chef of Kings," Auguste Escoffier's legacy lives on across the whole world, relayed by over 25,000 disciples. His Guide Culinaire, continually reprinted, is still the bible of every chef. In his native village of Villeneuve-Loubet, a few miles from Nice, his birthplace is now a Foundation and Museum of Culinary Art, created in 1966, and a regional Cultural Center bearing his name has been inaugurated. But maybe even more significant is the fact that, since 2011, the Auguste Escoffier Schools of Culinary Art created in the U.S. (Austin, Texas and Boulder, Colorado) contribute very successfully to perpetuate his teachings to enthusiastic professional students, including on-line.

And with his passion for cooking that made him write down his favorite recipes, very much in communion with Auguste's, somewhere along the line, Axel brought his little stone to the edifice.

Thank God that Karen found the notebook, so we can now all share those recipes, but even better, try them and enjoy them!

Axel during his last visit to Odense, Denmark.

Axel's graduation picture, larding needles, cutlery, and Paris map.

Introduction

By Karen Blumensaadt-Stoeckley

A Culinary Legacy – From Escoffier to Today

Sometime in the very distant past when I was about 18 years old, I was digging through an old chest in the attic of my maternal grandparents' farm garage. The chest had belonged to my paternal grandfather, who had immigrated from Denmark via France after a long hitch as an Escoffier trained chef in Paris and in the south of France. In 1904 he began writing a book of his recipes that I assume he had prepared at the various restaurants he had worked in. In this old ledger book, yellowed with age, was a treasure trove of recipes, all in French. At that time I had not come to realize my love of the culinary arts. But as I sat there in the dusty attic of the garage by a window offering afternoon sunshine that illuminated years of dust particles gently fluttering in the sun's rays, I decided that someday I would translate the book and publish the results. Not only did I find a book, but next to it in the chest was also a packet of handwritten letters of recommendation from various French restaurants where my grandfather had worked in the late 1800's.

Voila! I could visualize a book printed on paper that looked like the ledger with blue lines and red page numbers in a sepia tone. One page would show the beautiful, delicate hand script written with a gold tipped ink pen (included in the chest of goodies), and the opposite page would offer a modern day interpretation of the old recipe. His letters of recommendation would be scattered throughout the book along with pictures of his graduation from culinary school and when he was in service to the French Army in Montpellier at the officer's dining room. Also a few old menus from places he had worked were in the packet of letters and I thought this would be a great addition to the book. As I look back, I realize now that I had formed a lasting vision of how I thought the book would eventually look.

I carried that book almost around the world with me, always hoping the day would come when I could put aside the daily activities of life and concentrate on the translation and development of the book. When my husband John and I met in 1980, I shared the book with him and occasionally spoke to others about my dream over the years. Thus the time and the opportunity to make the book a reality had finally arrived and I took a much-needed sabbatical the fall and winter of 2012/13 to embark upon a dream almost 50 years old.

Karen Blumensaadt-Stoeckley

Most cookbooks focus on a specific theme. This book is different in that it has become an amalgamation of what my grandfather wrote over a hundred years ago and what Chef Max Callegari and I have interpreted and translated in the twenty-first century. Translating and writing this book in the small Provençal village of Les Arcs sur Argens, while living in a very old stone house in what is known as the Parage, has brought a flavor to the book that is somewhat different from Axel's original purpose. His was to simply record his recipes for his own professional use; ours is to bring the book to life with respect to his years as a chef, using the inspiration he provided, to offer recipes that will reflect the current French Provençal cuisine for home cooking.

First let's look at the origins of this tome. Axel Eugene Blumensaadt left his home of Odense, Denmark in late 1897 to travel to Paris, France to study the culinary arts. It appears he was only 16-years-old when he set out on this journey. On January 18th of that year he applied for a change of residence to France. I have often wondered by what means he traveled to Paris and what fears he may have felt to be alone in the journey. Family legend maintains he left at the dismay of his parents, who felt he should aspire to a higher goal in life than chef. Sitting at the foot of my bed is a handmade sea chest he built before leaving Odense. All his worldly belongings were contained in the chest and it survived his travels across the Atlantic twice, around France for numerous years, a few trips back to Denmark and a trip to California from Ohio.

He successfully completed his culinary studies after 18 months and went to Hyeres, France on the border of the Mediterranean Sea, west of St. Tropez. Here it is believed he served his first internship at the Grand Hotel du Parc during the winter of 1898 to the winter of 1899. He served as second chef with a recommendation written by Felix Suzanne, Directeur.

The letterhead of the Hotel stationary depicts the hotel, which today is a government building that still reflects the architectural grandeur of that bygone time with beautifully groomed lawns and pristine white stone columns.

Being near the water was not new to Axel, having been raised in Denmark where the sea touches the lives of most all the people of that country. But being this far away from his bourgeois home and the comforts that a successful family offers a young man could cause a severe case of homesickness. A chef's life in the late 1800's was not a comfy sort of occupation

Above: Stationary from the Grand Hotel du Parc.
Below: Axel's Book of recipes, shown with the gold tipped ink pen.

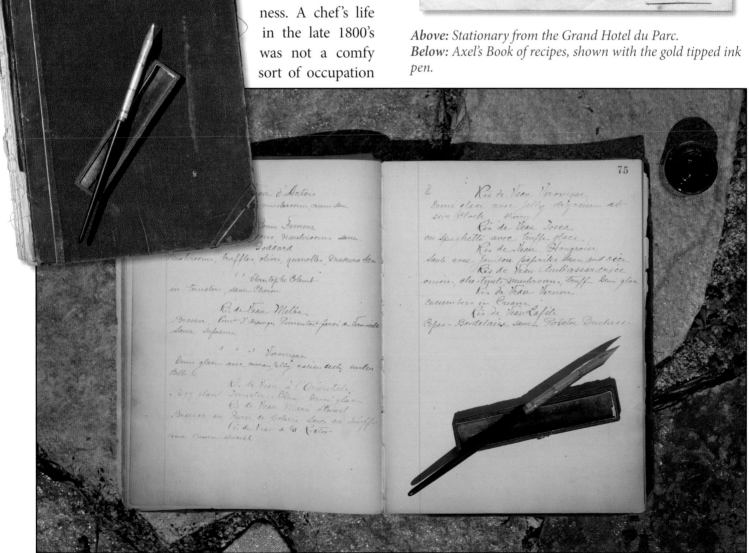

Axel's change of residency papers.

Above: Tickets for the 1900 Exposition Universelle. At left: Punch card for the exposition.

A young Axel

(not that is a piece of cake today)! Yet as we look at his picture as a new chef the image of a young, ambitious man shows him ready to venture into the world of the professional kitchen with determination, new found knowledge, and skill.

He was recruited to serve as Cuisine Garde Manager at the 1900 Exposition Universelle on the Champs Elysées in Paris. His punch card for entering the Exposition on a daily basis demonstrates a busy time in his career. He was only 20-years-old at that time. A lovely recommendation regarding his employment at the Exposition was written by Neils Larsen, Le Directeur of "La Feria" on November 12, 1900.

By April of 1901 Mr. Larsen had recruited Axel to move to Monte Carlo and work at the restaurant "La Feria" as Rotesseur Qualite, putting him back in the south of France near the sea. The influence the foods of the South of France had on his future style of cooking is demonstrated in his book. Today many of those same dishes are enjoyed throughout the area of Provence. It is suspected that Axel came directly under the influence of Auguste Escoffier, as most of the recipes in his book are those that originated with Escoffier. Since no records or lists of the over 2,000 young men Escoffier trained were ever maintained, there is no definite proof of this assumption, just the coincidence of the time frame and the written recipes.

Somewhere during the ensuing years until 1904 Axel took a trip to America, where his older brother Nicholai was living. On the voyage to America he met a charming young lady, Josephine Amelia Kramb, and her older sister and chaperone, Ida Kramb. A correspondence began but not in earnest as Axel had kitchens to conquer and people to feed. A menu from the St. James Hotel in Philadelphia attests to his steadfast resolve to prove his culinary talents. Wouldn't it be wonderful to dine on that cuisine today at the listed prices!

The St. James

Philadelphia

Dinner

BLUE POINTS, 25   LONG ISLAND SALTS, 30   CAPE MAY SALTS, 30
LYNN HAVENS, 30   SHREWSBURYS, 30

CELERY, 40   RADISHES, 15   OLIVES, 15   PIM OLAS, 30
SALTED ALMONDS, 25   LYON SAUSAGE, 45   CAVIAR, 40
TOMATO A LA ST. JAMES, 50   SARDINE A L'HUILE, 30
PIN MONEY PICKLES, 15

BEEF BROTH, A L'ANGLAISE, 40   25   CONSOMME, PRINCESSE, 35   20

BLUEFISH AU GRATIN, 75   FILET OF SOLE, NORMANDE, 80

CHICKEN FRICASSEE, PORT MAILLOT, $1.15
FILET MIGNON, A LA DICKINSON, $1.25   70
CALF'S HEAD, A LA POULETTE, 75

Fresh Mushrooms, 80   SALMI OF QUAIL, A LA DIANE, 90

Terrapin a la Maryland, $2.50

ROAST RIBS OF BEEF, 70   40   SPRING LAMB, MINT SAUCE, 70   40
ROAST TURKEY, CRANBERRY SAUCE, 85
BROILED SPRING TURKEY, $2.50 ½ $1.25   BROILED CELERY FED DUCK, $2.50

CHICKEN SALAD, 75   CRAB SALAD, 75   SWEETBREAD, $1.25
LOBSTER SALAD, 75   MACEDOINE 50   CHIFFONADE, 75   CUCUMBER, 40
TOMATO, 40   ROMAINE, 40   CHICOREE, 40   POTATO, 30
WATERCRESS, 30   ESCAROLE, 40   SALADE A LA ST. JAMES, 75

FRIED OYSTER PLANT, 40

Artichokes, 60   CAULIFLOWER, 50   SPINACH, 40   FRENCH PEAS, 85
BRUSSELS SPROUTS, 40   FRENCH ASPARAGUS, $1.00   NEW PEAS, 50
STUFFED TOMATOES, 40   STUFFED PEPPERS, 40   POTATOES ST. JAMES, 25
BOILED AND BAKED POTATOES, 20   SWEET POTATOES 25
BROILED SWEET POTATOES, 35   OYSTER BAY ASPARAGUS, 60

VIRGINIA HAM, 75

LEMON SOUFFLEE PUDDING, WINE SAUCE, 25   APPLE TARTELETTES, 25
CHOCOLATE OR VANILLA ECLAIR, 25   TUTTI FRUTTI ICE CREAM, 25
SHERRY WINE, JELLY, 25   SWISS MERINGUE, 25   COUPE, ST. JACQUES, 50
OMELETTE SOUFFLEE, 60
CHARLOTTE RUSSE, 25   CAFE PARFAIT, 30   ICE CREAM SANDWICH, 30
BISCUIT TORTONI, 30   VANILLA ICE CREAM, 25   CHOCOLATE ICE CREAM, 25
COFFEE ICE CREAM, 25   MERINGUE GLACE, 30   LALLA ROOKH,
LEMON ICE, 25   SORBET VARIES, 25   BAKED ALASKA, 60
ASSORTED FANCY CAKES, 20   BAR LE DUC, 40

Cheese—ROQUEFORT, 25   NEUFCHATEL, 25   STILTON, 30   SWISS,
BRIE 25   PHILADELPHIA CREAM. 25   CANADIAN CLUB, 25
PORT SALUT, 25   PONT L'EVEQUE, 25   CAMEMBERT, 25

ASSORTED FRUIT, 40   CAFE NOIR, 15

Wednesday, November 12, 1902.

In October 1904 to April 1905 (the same months I moved to France to work on his book, 107 years later) he had returned to Denmark and was first chef at the "Grand Hotel Copenhague." On that document he has written in pencil at the bottom, "…last time I was home as chef." And as it turned out, it was the last time he returned to Denmark. Also, it should be noted it was in 1904 that he began to write his book of recipes. Somewhere there was most likely a book from his school days and I get the sense this book was a more mature record of his recipes being served at his various places of employment. Remember, he had worked with older, more experienced chefs along the way and had developed skills and techniques not taught in the culinary school.

A second voyage to America was in the early fall of 1905 and on the ship, once again, was Josephine and sister Ida returning from yet another vacation in Europe.

At left: Menu from the St. James Hotel in Philadelphia.

This was a romance meant to be and the announcement of their wedding is shown here.

Axel and Josephine went to California, where she was a concert pianist and he a chef. At some point his brother Nicholai left the west coast and returned to Denmark and Axel and Josephine returned to Oak Harbor, Ohio, where the Kramb family owned a large dry goods store. Axel never again worked as a professional chef, but rather was consumed into the family business of retail. It is legend that the family ate very well and he dismissed the family cook so he might take over that responsibility to his liking.

In coming years Josephine gave the family two sons, Ernest and Christian, with Christian being my father. Neither pursued the culinary arts, but Chris and Ernie became accomplished sailors on the Great Lakes and Chris worked as a boat builder and talented carpenter, another skill that Axel also possessed.

Chef Max Callegari is the owner of Le Logis du Guetteur, an exceptional restaurant and hotel in the Medieval quarter of the Parage in Les Arcs sur Argens! Max consented to co-author this book with me throughout the winter, simply because he felt it would be fun. For his gracious assistance and esteemed ability in the culinary arts I will always be very grateful.

The handwriting in the book is beautiful as the included examples attest, but the old spellings and even some ingredients were a huge challenge to us both. Max never failed to translate and interpret Axel's meanings and directions. Additionally there are instances where Axel shifted to Danish, English and German. We tended to skip those references and stick to the French recipes.

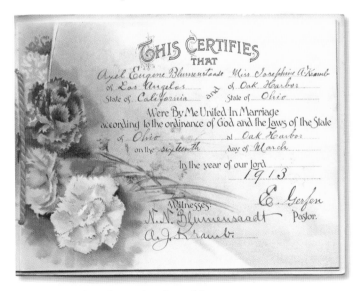

Axel and Josephine's wedding announcement.

Karen Blumensaadt-Stoeckley and Max Callegari

Le Logis du Guetteur, restaurant and hotel.

Max maintains that cooking is an art of the soul and baking is a precise science. With that philosophy he was able to add numerous ideas for interpreting Axel's recipes, providing today's home chef with delicious new twists on very old cuisine. Having said that, he also maintains that individual adjustments, within reason, allow the home cook to create new tastes and presentations of their own.

Many of the food photos in this book were shot at Max's restaurant and created in his kitchen. The evolution of the book was a pastime of interest to his staff throughout the winter and during the photo shoots in early spring. Their assistance is gratefully acknowledged.

My little sister Susan M. (Blumensaadt) Smith was very involved in the book from the USA and one short visit to Les Arcs in November. Her attention to detail and work on converting measurements from U.S. to metric has been of great assistance. With degrees in Library Science and Historical Administration, she was able to place Axel in age and time at various places throughout his career. It was a joy to work with her in creating this book of our grandfather and I am very grateful for her willingness to participate.

If the reader is looking for a lot of the tried and true Provençal recipes, they are not necessarily found in this book; there will be exceptions, of course.

About Provence and Axel's Recipes

While the old handwritten book lists numerous recipes from around the country of France, and a few from elsewhere, the main focus is on the cooking of Provence where he did most of his internship after his culinary training in Paris.

To try to adequately describe Provence would be a fool's task. It is a land of variables, a land of fragrances, a land of intrigue, of numerous cultures influenced for many centuries by Greeks, Italians, Portuguese, Spanish and even Brits. It is a land of rough, rocky terrain

and scrub grasses, including rosemary, thyme, sage and laurel all over the hillsides. It offers a seafood bounty from the sea. From the hills comes succulent lamb, pork, goat, veal and some beef. A Cavaillon melon can set your day right on a delicious route, or a course of the savory chèvre from the hill goats can end the perfect meal. Fresh figs from trees that grow wild are a bounty in the summer. Tender asparagus, both white and green, is plentiful in the village markets. Artichokes are available in numerous sizes and color from lime green to deep purple. Soupe de Poissons is on many menus with the traditional rouille sauce to spread on toasted baguette rounds.

Perched villages cling like a baby to its mother's breast on the sides of mountains and hills and you ask yourself, "What were they thinking? Ah-ha! …Protection from the bad guys and good vantage points to watch for the same." Terraces that date back hundreds of years rise up the hills like wide wale corduroy, constructed from millions of stones removed from the fields allowing the planting of vineyards and olive orchards. Specialties abound in the various Bistros, Cafes, Creperies, and fancy restaurants.

Eating is an art and a national pastime in France and certainly in Provence, where shops, banks, postal services, offices, and all commerce close promptly at noon for the mid-day meal and do not reopen until 2 or 3 p.m. Only restaurants are open and they are full of hungry folks who only had coffee and croissant for an early morning breakfast. This is the main meal of the day and it is revered by all, not to be rushed and usually accompanied by at least a demi pitchet of local wine from the cooperative; the plat du jour is on every menu daily.

I could wax poetically forever on this wonderful land of tradition, history, and very friendly people, but the book must go on and so it will, as we tie Axel's recipes to this inspiring land of divine ingredients and bountiful foods.

Door to Le Logis du Guetteur restaurant.

Consommé a l'alsacienne

Hors d'oeuvre Riches
Starters

$\mathcal{W}$e offer our version of Axel's hors d'oeuvre from one of the early pages of the book. Since many of his "recipes" are really just names of dishes, we have either researched recipes from his era and adapted them to today's kitchen, or offered our own versions of Povençal dishes.

Also included in this section are salads, egg dishes and consommés, all different types of starters to any meal.

In Provence the vibrant colors of the region are reflected in the foods, and without exception in the "starters" of most meals.

Sometimes just a dish of glistening olives ixed with ruby red pieces of pepper or a salad that boasts the fruits of that particular season. It is no secret that Picasso, Matisse, Signac, Cezanne and many other artists sought out this special light and presented their still life works of bountiful harvests in Provençal sunlight.

Appetizers

Herring is very typical seafood in France and often shows up as a starter on many menus. We suggest the two following recipes for tasty and different appetizers.

Canapés de Filet de Hareng

1¼ cups (296 ml) white wine
2 medium carrots thinly sliced
2 medium yellow onions thinly sliced
5-6 black peppercorns
2 bay leaves
Sprig of fresh tarragon or 2 tsp. (10 ml) dried
2 whole cloves
1 tsp. (5 ml) sea salt
8-10 fresh herrings (about 2 lbs. or 907 g)
½ cup (118 ml) cider vinegar
3 Tbsp. (44 ml) good quality olive oil
Optional: 2 tsp. (10 ml) juniper berries (to add to
   the simmering vegetables)

❊ In an enameled lined sauce pan (Le Creuset or Cousances) bring to a boil the wine, thinly sliced vegetables, herbs, and sea salt. Lower the heat and gently simmer for 20-30 minutes.

❊ Prepare the herring by removing the heads, tails, and fins. Scale them by drawing the back of a chef knife over the body until no more scales are evident. (A good suggestion is to do this in the bottom of your sink as the scales may tend to become a bit airborne.)

❊ Carefully slice open the belly if not already gutted and remove the innards. Wash the fish well and dry with a clean towel. Place the fish in a deep skillet.

❊ After the vegetables have simmered and are tender add the cider vinegar and bring back to a fast boil for 2 minutes.

❊ Ladle the vegetables and ¾ cup (177 ml) of the broth mixture over the herring in the skillet and simmer for 5-6 minutes.

❊ Remove the cloves and bay leaves and sprig of tarragon. Season lightly with salt and pepper. Pour the olive oil over the fish and vegetables and allow to completely cool.

❊ Place the fish and vegetables on a serving platter or shallow casserole dish and cover and refrigerate up to 3 or 4 days. Remove from the refrigerator at least two hours before serving. Surround the herring with toasted baguette slices rubbed with a garlic clove.

MAKES APPROXIMATELY 10 SERVINGS

As an alternative, you may purchase canned or packaged herring in olive oil and make the vegetable mixture and ladle it over the filets of herring that you have carefully placed on a large serving platter. If you can find smoked herring filets packaged in the cooler section of the market, these will be just fine. Should you prefer to use canned herring buy only the best available and use two or three cans for this recipe. Serve as above. You do not need to hold these for a few days before serving.

MAKES APPROXIMATELY 14-16 SERVINGS

A Second Herring Selection

2 lbs. (907 g) fresh herring cleaned as above or
   packaged filets
2 Tbsp. (30 ml) unsalted butter
2 Yukon potatoes boiled and well chilled
2 medium yellow onions thinly sliced
¾ cup (177 ml) white vinegar
3-4 Tbsp. (44-59 ml) olive oil
Toasted Baguette slices (as many slices as herring)
2 cloves garlic halved
2-3 Tbsp. (30-44 ml) olive oil (additional)
Fresh chervil finely chopped

❊ Melt the butter in a nonstick skillet until foamy and sauté the herring for 1-2 minutes per side, turning them gently. Do not crowd the skillet. Lift herring to a platter to drain. Reserve cooked juices.

❊ Place the onions in the same skillet and add the white vinegar. Simmer until all the vinegar has evaporated or been absorbed into the onions and they are "dry."

❊ Slice the baguette in ¼ inch slices and lightly brush with olive oil and rub with the cut garlic slices. Toast in a 375°F (190°C) oven until golden and slightly crispy. Be careful not to over brown.

❊ Slice the cold boiled potato in thin slices and place on top of each toasted baguette slice. Top with a small spoonful of the cooked onion and lay a herring across the onion topping.

❊ Drizzle with the olive oil and sprinkle with just a touch of finely chopped chervil. Serve at room temperature.

MAKES APPROXIMATELY 20-25 SERVINGS
DEPENDING ON THE SIZE OF THE HERRING

Barquette de Crevettes

SMALL SHRIMP IN PASTRY BOATS

These dainty shrimp appetizers are sure to please and will be quickly consumed, so make plenty. Alternatively, for a sit-down dinner you can serve as an appetizer by placing one of each filling on a small leaf of lettuce on an appetizer plate. The boat shaped pastry molds are generally made of tin and available in gourmet shops. They are about 3 inches long and one inch wide.

1 lb. (454 g) small salad shrimp
Fresh chopped parsley for garnish
⅓ cup each of Aioli, Melba Cocktail Sauce and
*   herbed Mayonnaise (page 147)*
Savory Pastry Crust (page 135)

❀ Cook the salad shrimp in salted boiling water until pink, taking care not to overcook or the shrimp will be tough.

❀ Drain and run under cold water. Reserve in the refrigerator until needed. Frequently these tiny shrimp are available precooked and frozen. In that case simply thaw and toss with just a touch of lemon juice to refresh.

❀ Roll out the pastry dough on a floured surface. Using a 3 inch round biscuit cutter, cut as many rounds as possible. Gather up the dough scraps and reroll and repeat cutting circles.

❀ Gently press the dough into molds. Prick dough with a fork and set on a baking sheet. To keep their shape fill molds with dried beans or pastry beads. Bake in a preheated 375°F (190°C) oven until pastry is golden brown and not translucent looking. Keep in mind you will be filling these boats with some sauce and four or five small shrimp.

❀ All of the above may be done one or two days ahead and the boats can be kept in an air tight plastic container until ready to fill. Do not refrigerate baked boats.

❀ Fill the bottom of the boats with your choice of sauces. Place four or five small shrimp attractively in the boats. Sprinkle lightly with finely chopped parsley. Serve as a passed appetizer, on an appetizer buffet, or for a sit down dinner; they are a finger food however they are served.

MAKES ABOUT 25-30 SERVINGS

Lasange de Saumon fumé glacé

SMOKED SALMON ROLLS

This simple but elegant appetizer can be made early in the day of serving and refrigerated. You may come up with your own ideas of flavoring for the filling, using chopped capers or finely minced red onion as a suggestion.

1 lb. (454 g) thinly sliced smoked salmon at room temperature
1 cup (237 ml) heavy whipping cream, whipped stiff
⅓ cup (70 ml) sour cream at room temperature
½ cup (118 ml) assorted fresh herbs, such as thyme, savory, oregano, or tarragon, finely minced, including some mint leaves
1 tsp. (5 ml) ground coriander

✾ Carefully fold the sour cream into the whipped cream. Add all the herbs and gently fold into the cream mixture. Set aside.

✾ Using a thin knife blade separate slices of the salmon. Evenly spread the cream herb mixture on the slices.

✾ Roll the slices up like cannelloni (tube) and lay them on a cookie sheet with the seam side down. Refrigerate at least one hour.

✾ Using a very sharp non-serrated knife, slice the rolls into 1 inch bite size pieces like a jelly roll.

✾ Place on a serving platter and garnish with slices of lemon. Sprinkle with finely chopped parsley.

MAKES APPROXIMATELY 50 PINWHEELS

Oeufs durs garnis de Caviar frais

EGGS WITH CAVIAR

A sophisticated version of deviled eggs with the option to be creative to suit your own taste. You can count on these becoming favorites of family and friends.

6 large eggs
4-5 cups (946-1183 ml) ice
½ cup (118 ml) real mayonnaise (not salad dressing)
½ cup (118 ml) heavy whipping cream, whipped stiff
1 tsp. (5 ml) finely chopped chervil
2 Tbsp. (30 ml) caviar or salmon, trout or lump fish eggs

✾ Boil the eggs for 9 -10 minutes in water with a little white vinegar, (makes peeling easier).

✾ Immediately remove from the heat, drain and run under cold water and put in the ice to quickly cool the eggs. Allow to sit in the ice water for at least 5 minutes.

✾ Carefully peel the eggs and cut in half lengthwise.

✾ Remove the yolk and push through a fine sieve into a medium mixing bowl.

✾ Beat in the mayonnaise well and gently fold in the whipped cream, the chervil, and the caviar. Chill for 30 minutes to allow to set.

✾ Place a scoop of the yolk filling in the center of each white half. (Cutting a very thin slice off the bottom of the whites will allow them to sit flat on your serving platter.)

✾ Top each with just a very small sprig of the chervil. Serve chilled.

MAKES 12 SERVINGS

For a Peasant's version you could substitute finely chopped Kalamata olives for the caviar. Additionally you can use chopped capers, chopped pimentos, or very finely chopped crisp bacon. Whatever you add should be finely chopped and do not use too much as to overwhelm the flavor. Make an assorted platter of these stuffed eggs. However, nothing beats the caviar!

Josephine's Pâté

This recipe came down through the family and still today is a favorite of many. Josephine was Axel's lovely wife and I am not sure when this began to be called "Josephine's" but that is how it stands today. The recipe was adapted many years ago to the food processor by my mother, Marguerite. It is a pâté that can be served in small pots or in a terrine, or made in a small loaf pan lined with plastic wrap to allow it to be gently lifted out while chilled. Done in this manner it can be sliced and presented on individual plates with crostini, cornichons and a dab of Dijon mustard or confit of onion. If serving as an appetizer for a cocktail party, allow it to be at room temperature for ease in spreading.

Since coming to Les Arcs I have found little tan, paper loaf cups in the baking section of the HyperU grocery center and when I make up a big batch I make small "take away" loaves for guests who have enjoyed the flavor. Since it lasts up to three weeks in the refrigerator, it is a convenient little departing gift. Little glass jars or pots could also be used. Rene and Arlette, from Lorgues, and Dottie Brown Murray from Louisiana, Missouri are my biggest fans of this Pâté!

6 celery ribs w/leaves if available
12 whole peppercorns
12 cups (2839 ml) water
2 Tbsp. (30 ml) salt
1 bay leaf
2 lbs. (907 g) chicken livers drained
  and washed
1 tsp. (5 ml) cayenne pepper
1½ lbs. (680 g) of unsalted butter
2 tsp. (10 ml) ground nutmeg
1 tsp. (5 ml) ground cloves
¾ cup (177 ml) roughly chopped yellow
  onion
3 garlic cloves
½ cup (118 ml) Calvados or brandy
½ cup (118 ml) heavy cream
1 tsp. (5 ml) salt
1 tsp. (5 ml) fine ground black pepper
1 cup (237 ml) dried currants or
  golden raisins

❋ Chop the celery ribs in thirds and add to the 12 cups (2839 ml) of water in a large kettle or sauce pan. Add the 2 tablespoons (30 ml) salt and the bay leaf. Bring to a boil and reduce the heat and simmer for 10 minutes.

❋ Add the chicken livers and bring back to a slow bubble simmer. Simmer on medium low heat for 12 minutes.

❋ Drain the livers, discard the celery ribs and peppercorns, and immediately place in a food processor with the steel blade in place. Place the butter, cut into pieces, on top of the hot livers. Add all the remaining ingredients EXCEPT the currants and process until very smooth about 5 to 6 minutes.

❋ Add the currants and pulse 3 or 4 times. If using raisins pulse 5 to 6 times to only chop the raisins and not puree them.

❋ Pour into a terrine or pots and refrigerate overnight or at least 8 hours. I always garnish the top with either the currants or raisins, just in the middle.

MAKES ABOUT 6 CUPS (1420 ML)

Moules Marinière

MUSSELS PROVENÇAL

Since this recipe has been a favorite of guests at The Eagle's Nest, we offer that modern day version for your enjoyment.

2 Tbsp. (30 ml) olive oil
5 large garlic cloves finely minced
2 large tomatoes skinned, seeded, and chopped
2 lbs. (907 g) fresh cleaned mussels or frozen
  mussels
¾ cup (177 ml) dry white wine
¼ cup (59 ml) chopped parsley
Salt and pepper to taste

✤ In a deep kettle heat the olive oil and add the garlic. Cook for one minute over medium high heat. Do not brown the garlic or it will make the mussels bitter.

✤ Add the chopped tomato and cook for 2 minutes. Add the salt and pepper and the parsley.

✤ Add the cleaned mussels and the white wine. Cover and steam for 3 to 4 minutes, shaking the pan to coat the mussels in the wine mixture.

✤ Divide the mussels between 4 deep soup dishes and ladle the tomato wine broth evenly over the mussels.

✤ Serve with plenty of warm French bread for soaking up the broth in the bottom of the bowl. If a mussel does not open, discard it, as it is not fresh.

SERVES 4

Here is also an idea: If you add a large spoonful of cream you will get another recipe that we call "Moules Poulette."

Brandade de Morue

SALT COD PUREE ON TOAST POINTS

This is such a delicious dish and well worth the effort. I teach this dish in my Provençal cooking classes and it shows up in Axel's book, so it is a natural to share here. I first tried this dish in a waterfront café in Cassis many years ago and that experience sold me on this very old recipe, still as good today as it was 100 years ago.

1.5 lbs. (680 g) cod filets OR 1 lb. (454 g) dried salted cod
1 cup (237 ml) virgin olive oil
¾ cup (180 ml) half and half or whole milk
3 medium garlic cloves pressed or crushed and minced
½ tsp. (2.5 ml) white pepper
4 slices white sourdough bread, crusts removed

❋ If using dried salt cod, begin a few days in advance. Put the cod in a glass or non-reactive bowl and cover with cold water. Cover bowl with plastic wrap and refrigerate overnight.

❋ Change the water 3 or 4 times in 24 hours.

❋ To prepare for serving, place the cod in a saucepan and cover with water and bring to a slow boil and simmer until the cod has tenderized, about 20 minutes.

❋ Drain and cool and remove any skin. Flake the cod as finely as possible in a bowl.

❋ If using fresh cod, pat filets well with kosher salt or fine sea salt on both sides. Place on a wire rack over a sheet pan. Put into a warm 145°F (63°C) oven for 4 hours. Open oven door and allow to cool for 2 hours on the rack.

❋ Over a mixing bowl flake cod as finely as possible with your fingers.

❋ In two separate saucepans, warm half of the olive oil and the half and half in one and set aside off the heat.

❋ In the second pan, using low heat, warm the other half of the oil.

❋ Add the flaked cod to the pan and mash well with a wooden spoon into the oil, slowly adding tablespoons of the oil/milk mixture and continuing to stir and mash until all the oil and milk becomes absorbed. Season with white pepper.

Cut the bread slices in 4 triangles each and sauté in 1 tablespoon of foaming butter until crispy and golden. Spread the Brandade on each triangle. Serve warm.

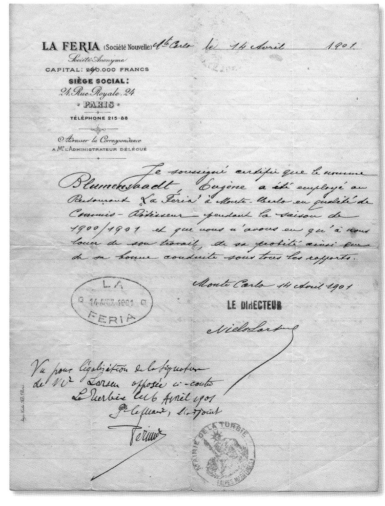

Right: Axel's reference for La Feria.

Artichauts a la Barigoule
(Provençal Way)

ARTICHOKES BARIGOULE

4 small to medium size artichokes
2 Tbsp. (30 ml) olive oil
3 garlic cloves minced
4 slices thick bacon, diced
2 tsp. (10 ml) oregano
½ cup (118 ml) dry white wine

❈ Wash the artichokes well. Cut off the bottom stem and about ½ inch of the top.

❈ Cut off the sharp tip of each leaf with scissors. Cut each artichoke into fourths lengthwise and remove the pith (the furry center) from each piece. If using small long stemmed chokes do not cut in fourths.

❈ Sauté the bacon pieces in the olive oil until almost crisp.

❈ Add the garlic and continue to sauté for one minute.

❈ Add the artichokes cut sides down and sauté 2 minutes.

❈ Add the white wine, cover and simmer 15 minutes.

❈ Place on a heated serving platter sprinkled with grated Parmesan cheese.

❈ Spoon the bacon and garlic bits over the artichoke pieces evenly.

❈ Spear with toothpicks. Serve warm. You can surround the artichokes with toasted crostini rounds to allow your guests a "mini plate" for each serving.

Note: Our photo shows using just the bottoms with the long stalk kept intact. Either method is acceptable.

Marinated Olives and Peppers

The marketplaces are the most exciting places to select olives for munching and appetizers. Many varieties and ways of marinating olives are offered by the vendors. My artist husband does not understand why a bowl and toothpicks are not offered at the end of the table, allowing customers to just graze! Having a constant supply of marinated olives at home is easy and less expensive. This is how I keep a good supply on hand at all times.

3 cups (710 ml) Kalamata olives in brine
2 cups (473 ml) jumbo stuffed olives in brine
1 cup (237 ml) mild banana peppers in brine
Rind of one small lemon cut in strips
5 peeled and slightly smashed garlic cloves
1 cup + (237 ml) good quality olive oil
1 level Tbsp. (15 ml) Herbs de Provence

❊ Drain the olives and peppers very well.

❊ Place in alternating layers with the lemon rind, garlic and herbs in a clear glass jar with a tight fitting lid.

❊ Pour in the olive oil to completely cover all ingredients. Cover and allow to marinate for two days before serving.

❊ As the content dwindles you may add more olives and peppers, garlic and fresh lemon zest. Add oil as needed.

Pickled Onion Confit

This tasty condiment is delicious served with Patè Maison, Josephine's Patè, grilled meats and poultry. It keeps well in the refrigerator for weeks in a covered glass jar. Also it makes a nice gift when canned in decorative small jars.

6 red onions, very thinly sliced
1 cup (237 ml) red wine vinegar
2 cups (473 ml) dry red wine
1 cup (237 ml) granulated sugar
1 cinnamon stick
5 whole cloves
1 bay leaf
½ tsp. (2.5 ml) salt

❊ In a large non-reactive saucepan, place all the liquid ingredients and the sugar. Bring to a boil and stir to dissolve the sugar.

❊ Add the cinnamon stick, bay leaf and the cloves and boil for 5 minutes.

❊ Add the onion and salt and lower the heat to simmer. Simmer for 40 minutes or until the liquid has reduced to turn to a shiny, thick sauce on the onions.

❊ Remove the bay leaf and cinnamon stick. The cloves may stay in the confit until serving time.

❊ Cool and place in a glass jar and cover tightly until ready to serve. Serve at room temperature.

MAKES APPROXIMATELY 2 CUPS (473 ML)

Marinated Olives and Peppers

Pâté Maison

My artist husband has his favorites and this is at the top. Axel made various types of pâté, and we share this full flavored one with you. Pâtés are a staple in the boucherie in the villages and towns, with each butcher having his own signature dish. Delicious as a starter in slices on a small plate with cornichons, Dijon mustard or whole grain mustard, pickled onion confit and toast points or crostini rounds. Le Creuset makes a wonderful Pâté Terrine just right for this and it has a tight fitting lid for storage, if you are lucky to have any left over.

1 lb. (454 g) lean pork shoulder
1 lb. (454 g) pork sausage
1 lb. (454 g) boneless veal
1 lb. (454 g) beef stew meat
1 cup (237 ml) chicken liver
2 boneless skinless chicken breast
⅓ cup (79 ml) brandy or Cognac
3 eggs, beaten
3 tsp. (15 ml) salt
4 cloves garlic
1 tsp. (5 ml) ground clove minced
½ tsp. (2.5 ml) ground nutmeg
1 tsp. (5 ml) white pepper
½ cup (118 ml) shelled pistachio nuts
2 tsp. (10 ml) Herbs de Provence
4 or 5 bay leaves
6 slices smoked bacon

❀ Cut the meats into 1 inch (2.5 cm) chunks and place in a food processor in small batches and pulse to roughly chop. Empty into a big mixing bowl and repeat until all the meat is chopped, adding a small portion of the chicken livers to each batch to chop and blend with the meats.

❀ Add the brandy, eggs, salt, garlic cloves, spices and herbs and blend well. Fold in the nuts.

❀ Line the terrine with the slices of bacon alternating from side to side, allowing the bacon to hang over the edges of the terrine. You will have three slices hanging over on each side.

❀ Pack the meat mixture into the terrine tightly and tamp down to eliminate any air pockets. Top with bay leaves. Fold the alternating slices of bacon over the top of the meat. Tuck any long ends into the sides.

❀ Cover the terrine tightly with a double layer of aluminum foil and then put on the lid if your terrine has one.

❀ Place the terrine in a Bain Marie (larger pan half filled with water) and place in a preheated 350°F (177°C) oven and bake for 2 hours.

❀ Remove the foil and bake, uncovered for 30 minutes. Remove from oven leaving in the Bain Marie to be weighted down.

❀ Cover a regular building brick with foil and place directly on top of the meat mixture. Allow to sit for two or three hours until completely cooled. There will be a spillover of fat juices when you do this, into the Bain Marie. By weighting the pâté down it will be compact and slice nicely.

❀ Remove the brick and cover the terrine and refrigerate. This will keep for up to 10 days if refrigerated and the bacon and fat is left on the pâté. Slice chilled and allow to sit at room temperature for 20 to 30 minutes before serving for best taste results.

Consommés divers

1) Consommé a l'alsacienne
petits ravioli fare de foigras, Choucroute
blanchi cuite au Consommé.

2) Consommé Andalouse
Timbale Soubises, Quenelles a la tomate
et Œuf poché.

3) Consommé Bartholdi
Legumes coupe en petits losanges
pluche de Cerfueil.

4) Consommé Brillant – Savarin
Timbale de Volaille au Soubisée,
carrots, celery et champinon en
Julienne et crouton rond.

5) Consommé Berchoux
Con-- de Gibees. Filet de Caille en Julienne
Langeu. fet un Appareie avez carcasses des
cailles, velouté, œuf et pochée dans de petits
moules.

6) Consommé Brésilien
Consommé de Sagou mélange avec
(la Soup ou) tomate.

Consommés

One hundred years ago consommés were served as the starter for almost all formal dinners. A consommé is a clear light broth made from chicken, veal or beef. The substance in the broth is varied and here again you have the opportunity to be creative with whatever you have on hand. You have the choice to make a consommé the traditional way or you may elect to purchase a good quality broth ready-made. We offer the traditional recipe and you may enjoy trying your hand at this method at least once for the experience. In any case the quantity of broth in each recipe is given for using either method.

Poultry Consommé

To make a consommé the traditional way will require time and patience, but the end result is delightful and unparalleled in flavor, not to mention your personal sense of accomplishment. The chicken carcasses can be created by cutting away the breast, and thigh of a fresh chicken. Save that meat for another meal or roast it with herbs and sea salt to julienne in your consommé later. If you use two small chickens you will have sufficient legs for both the broth and the clarification process.

The Stock

1 large or two small chicken carcasses, including the legs and wings, all fat and skin removed
1 large carrot roughly chopped
1 celery stalk roughly chopped
1 white onion roughly chopped
2 whole peeled garlic cloves
Sprigs of fresh parsley
2 bay leaves
1 Tbsp. (15 ml) black peppercorns

❧ In a very large heavy bottom kettle put 4 quarts of cold water. Add the carcasses and boil for 15 minutes. If there is any fat that rises to the top, skim it off.

❧ Add the legs and all the vegetables and herbs. Keep on a simmer for about 2 hours, uncovered. The liquid will reduce by about ⅓ of the volume.

❧ Allow to cool slightly and pour through a fine strainer back into a clean kettle.

Clarification process

2 chicken legs, skin removed and meat finely chopped
1 carrot finely chopped
1 celery stalk finely chopped
3 green onions finely chopped using about 2 inches of the green top only

Note: the above four ingredients may be finely chopped in a food processor, taking care not to purée. Process individually.

1 Tbsp. (15 ml) black peppercorns
2 Roma tomatoes seeded and chopped
2 or 3 sprigs of fresh parsley
2 egg whites, beaten until frothy but not stiff

❧ In a separate kettle place all the above clarification ingredients and add 2 cups of the strained stock. Simmer for 5 minutes until just incorporated together.

❧ Pour the mixture into the strained stock and stir well to incorporate only. Do not boil but bring to a simmer over low heat. The top of the stock will form what is called a "raft" that carries all the impurities out of the stock.

❧ Simmer the stock for 1 hour and carefully remove the raft with a ladle and discard. Since the stock does not get strained at this point, keeping the raft to one side of the kettle allows easier removal of it as needed.

❧ After the stock has simmered for at least one hour it is now time to strain the stock through double cheesecloth lining a strainer.

❧ Should there be any fat floating on top of the strained stock it can be removed with dry cheesecloth that you lay gently on the top of the stock and quickly pull away. Plain white or natural paper towel may also be used. Season the stock with sea salt*.

Now your stock is ready for any of the many additions offered here or your own combinations. You should have about 6 or 7 cups (1420-1656 ml)

*Sea salt does not have iodine in it as does normal table salt, which will cloud your stock.

Consommé Cincinnati

1 cup (237 ml) each: tiny mini carrots, diced
turnips, potato cut into round balls (use a melon
baller)
3 cups (710 ml) consommé stock, salted to taste
4 pieces of sliced baguette, toasted
½ cup (118 ml) shredded Gruyère cheese

Consommé a l'alsacienne

❋ In a pot of sea salted boiling water cook the vegetables until tender but still a bit crisp to the bite. Do not overcook. Drain well.

❋ Bring the stock to a soft boil and add the vegetables. Simmer for 4 minutes. Taste for seasoning and add white pepper and sea salt if needed.

❋ Heat the broiler. Place the toasted baguette slices on a cookie sheet and top with equal portions of the cheese. Place under the broiler and melt the cheese, watching carefully as not to brown or burn the cheese or bread.

❋ Ladle the soup into warm soup plates and distribute the vegetables evenly across the plates. Top with the cheese crostini and serve immediately.

SERVES 4

Consommé a l'alsacienne

In French, "Choucroute" means cabbage or sauerkraut. For this very old recipe you probably cannot find ravioli filled with foie gras unless you decide to tackle the project and make your own. We suggest using a purchased ravioli with mushrooms but not any cheese.

3 cups (710 ml) stock
2 cups (473 ml) purchased mini ravioli
½ head green cabbage
1 cup (237 ml) white wine
½ cup (118 ml) white vinegar
3 or 4 juniper berries (optional)

❋ Cut the cabbage into very thin strips (almost a shredded form) about 4 inches long. Place the wine and vinegar and juniper berries if using, in a non-reactive saucepan and bring to a boil.

❋ Add the sliced cabbage and bring back to a boil for 15 minutes or until very tender. Drain well.

❋ In a clean saucepan add the stock and bring to a gentle boil. Add the ravioli and cook until tender. Add the cabbage strips and bring back to a gentle boil. Taste for seasoning and add white pepper and sea salt if needed.

❋ Ladle into warmed soup plates and divide the ravioli and cabbage evenly.

SERVES 4

Should you have access to foie gras, a pot of it with toast rounds would be a nice compliment.

If you have access to fresh currants, these go nicely as an accent in the broth. Drop in the simmering broth for just 2 or 3 minutes before ladling into bowls.

Variations for Consommé

If you happen to have left over chicken, turkey, veal or beef, you may slice the cold meat in very thin strips and place in the simmering broth. If using beef be sure you are using a beef broth, not poultry.

To any of these you may add thinly sliced (length wise) scallions, leeks, carrots, mushrooms, fresh spinach, baby peas, julienne of haricot vert, or any other vegetable you desire. The main idea is to have all your ingredients sliced very thin and delicately. You may also add small potato slices or balls if you have previously cooked the potato in salted boiling water. Do not attempt to cook the potato in the broth or it will turn cloudy. Winter squash such as hubbard, acorn or butternut can also make a lovely consommé with the addition of julienned (thin sliced) ham or turkey. Be sure to precook the squash, chill and cut into small squares or dice. In any case add your ingredients to the simmering broth just prior to serving and always use a warmed soup plate. Normally you need only simmer the additional ingredients for 4 or 5 minutes to cook through unless it was previously cooked, then a nice simmer for 3 minutes should suffice.

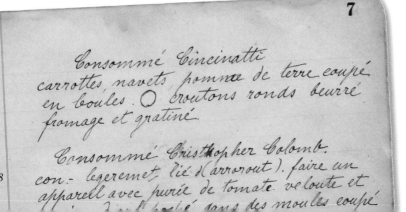

Seafood in Consommé

You have the same opportunities to add seafood to your broth. Small shrimp with scallions or leeks make a nice presentation and is delicious. A quenelle of seafood is also nice in broth. A recipe for quenelles follows. Lobster bites that have been sautéed in butter and drained well with small diced fresh tomato, seeds and pulp removed, are delicious in broth. Seasoning of thyme or tarragon works well with seafood.

A quenelle is a form of dumpling that is poached. It can be made with seafood, poultry, veal or any light colored meat. The recipe here is for seafood but with a little imagination you can substitute other meats. We are recommending using a choux mixture in your quenelles. That is a form of pastry that is used in many different French dishes including puffs for desserts filled with rich creams or jams. For this recipe we are using fewer eggs than in a normal choux pastry to allow the meat of the fish to hold it together better.

To begin the quenelles

2 lbs. (907 g) white fish such as cod, tilapia,
 haddock or salmon if you prefer
¾ cup (177 ml) water
3 Tbsp. (44 ml) unsalted butter
3 Tbsp. (44 ml) flour
2 large eggs
3 egg whites
¾ cup (177 ml) heavy cream
½ tsp. (2.5 ml) ground nutmeg
2 tsp. (10 ml) salt
White pepper to taste

❋ Clean the fish removing the fins, skin, scales and bones. Reserve those parts to make a court bullion for another day.

❋ Cut the fish into small pieces and place in a food processor and puree them until they completely form a paste.

❋ Working this mix thru a fine sieve will assure you a better product in the end. Place the mixture in a metal bowl and chill very well. It must be quite cold to complete the quenelle.

❋ While the fish mixture is chilling:

❋ In a stainless saucepan bring ¾ cup (177 ml) of water to a boil. Add the butter, flour, the whole eggs, and salt and pepper.

❋ Stir quickly with a wooden spoon until all is incorporated and the mixture begins to pull away from the sides of the pan. Set aside and allow to cool. You may brush the mixture with a touch of melted butter to keep it from forming a crust on the outside of the ball of pastry.

❋ Beat the egg whites until just soft and about to form peaks. Do not over beat them or they will separate in the quenelle. Fold them into the chilled fish mixture and beat very well again using a wooden spoon.

❋ Begin to beat in the choux dough, adding about 2 tablespoons (30 ml) per addition and beat well between each addition. After all the choux mixture is incorporated begin to add the cream, a little at a time until all is added. Add the salt and pepper and nutmeg and beat well.

❋ Bring 4 cups (946 ml) of broth to a simmer. Using two teaspoons dipped into a pan of boiling water, scoop one spoonful of the mixture and round the top with the other spoon, creating an oval shaped dome. Drop into the simmering broth. Dip the teaspoons in the boiling water before forming each quenelle.

❋ Allow to simmer 6 to 8 minutes or until firm. If a quenelle breaks up carefully remove it from the broth with a slotted spoon. If that problem continues beat another egg white into the mixture and add 1 more teaspoon (5 ml) of salt. Chill again before continuing. Allow 3 or 4 quenelles per serving.

❋ An addition of finely chopped scallions, green part included, is nice with this dish. Add them just before finishing and allow to simmer with the quenelles for 2 minutes. Ladle into heated bowls and serve immediately. Serves 4 to 6

❋ Finally, if you wish to have a more substantial soup, do not hesitate to add ½ cup (118 ml) of heavy cream to the broth at the last moment. Do not boil; just heat through completely to a simmer. Adjust seasonings to compensate for the addition. Proceed with any of the ingredients you prefer.

Chicken Consommé

2 chicken breasts
1 bay leaf
4-5 black peppercorns
2 medium carrots cut into fine julienne pieces 4
* inches (10 cm) long*
2 stalks of celery cut into fine julienne pieces 4
* inches (10 cm) long*
1 leek cut into very thin 4 inch (10 cm) strips
4 cups (946 ml) clear chicken consommé
Finely chopped fresh parsley

❁ Poach the chicken breasts in salted simmering water with the whole peppercorns and bay leaf for 30 minutes.

❁ Remove and allow to cool.

❁ Add the carrots and poach in the liquid for 5 minutes. Remove and keep hot.

❁ Add the celery and poach 3 minutes. Remove and keep warm.

❁ Add the leeks and poach 5 minutes. Remove and keep warm.

❁ Cut the chicken breasts into thin 4 inch (10 cm) strips to match the vegetables.

❁ Bring the consommé almost to a boil and ladle into heated bowls (it is very important that the bowls are heated). Divide the chicken breasts between the bowls evenly laying the strips all going in the same direction.

❁ Add the vegetables, divided evenly. Top with a sprinkle of the parsley and serve immediately.

SERVES 4 GENEROUSLY
OR 6 IN SMALLER BOWLS

Note: When heating the consommé, you can add
¾ cup (180 ml) of preheated heavy cream that
has a dash of cayenne pepper added. Be sure
not to boil at any point. Add additional salt
to compensate for the addition of a liquid.
Continue as directed and serve a nice cream
soup, enough for 6 small soup bowls.

Les Arcs at sunset.

Salade Kinge Edward

Pomme d'arbre Celerie e—. Bananes en Julien
Raisen fresh (Graps.) Sans Mayonaise des œufs des
(ohny th fok.) Citron et Vin de Sherry french Dressing
Decore avec Rain blanc
et rouge et de Noi hashi

Lettre
blanc
noi
rouge

blanc

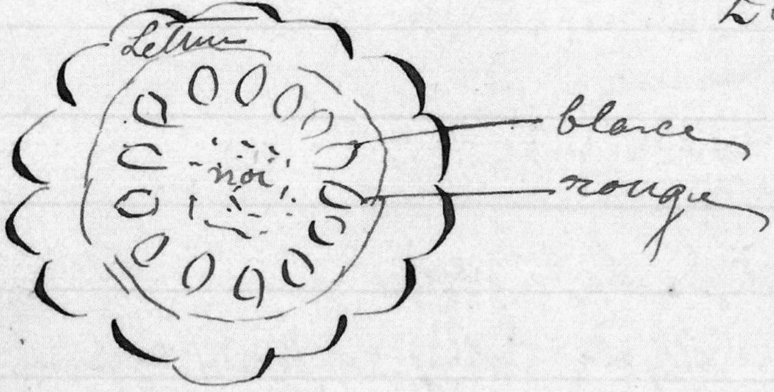

Salade a la Taft

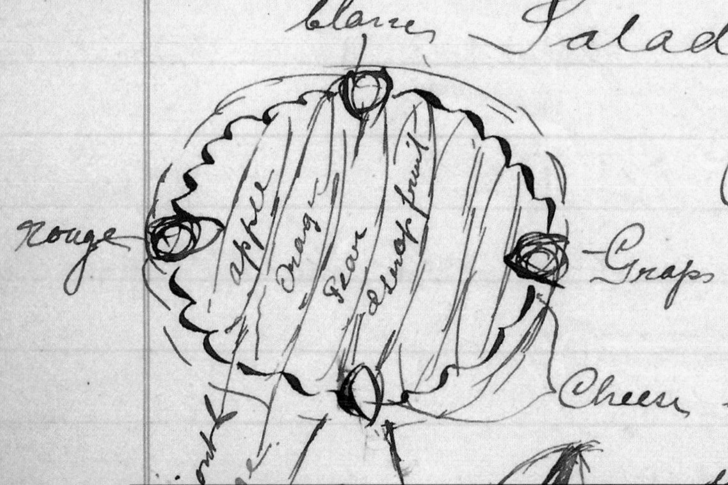

rouge

apple
Orange
Pear
Grape fruit

Cœur de Lettre Graps fruits
Graps Orange pomme d'arbre, Poire
rouge et vert piment
Cheesn decore avec fromage de Crem
et Raisn french dres rouge

fruit
Mayon

Just a word or two about salads in France and more specifically in Provence.

The first time a visitor to France orders a salad they are usually thinking they are going to receive a typical side salad and are surprised to receive what is considered a full meal platter. Most salads are composed and include numerous different ingredients, often including a poached egg. Here we are offering a bevy of ideas taken from Axel's book and including a few of our own favorites.

As for a simple tossed American style salad you may wish to employ one of the simple dressings offered at the end of this book. A true French dressing is not orange in a bottle but a mélange of oil, vinegar, salt, pepper and Dijon mustard whisked together to make a smooth, creamy sauce to drizzle over crisp greens. Thus when we refer to French dressing this is what we are expecting you to use.

As for the composed salads you may wish to use them for a luncheon with a cup of consommé or bisque and served with a crunchy baguette or brioche roll. For evening supper a composed salad is always a good departure from the standard fare of meat and potatoes or pasta, and is a delicious alternative when one is watching their calorie and fat intake but wanting a decent meal.

The first three salads are primarily fruit based and are lovely as a main course or to be served before or after a main entrée of meat or fish.

Salade a la Taft

This is a composed salad that may be presented as one large salad to serve four or arranged on individual plates for four.

*3 cups (710 ml) assorted tender
  lettuce greens in small pieces*
*1 grapefruit in sections
  (membrane removed)*
*2 oranges in sections, (membrane
  removed)*
½ cup (118 ml) red grapes
½ cup (118 ml) green grapes
1 red pear
1 yellow pear
*1 apple cut into thin wedges with
  skin on*
½ cup (118 ml) golden raisins

*2-3 oz. (59-79 ml) log fresh chevre cheese sliced
  into ¼ inch rounds*
¾ cup (177 ml) French dressing (page 143)

✤ Cut the citrus fruit over a small bowl to catch the juice drippings and set the citrus sections aside on paper towels to continue to drain.

✤ Place greens on a large round chilled serving platter, completely covering the platter with about a two inch margin around the edge. Refrigerate until ready to assemble the salad.

✤ Wash the grapes and remove from the stems. Set aside.

✤ Slice the pears into thin long wedges, removing the cores. With a pastry brush gently brush the pear slices with the reserved citrus juice to keep the pears from browning.

✤ Repeat this process with the apple (leaving the red skin on the apple).

✤ Assembly: On the platter of lettuce begin by placing the cheese rounds around the outer edge of the platter slightly overlapping edges.

✤ Every three rounds intersperse with red grapes and alternate with green grapes.

✤ Create rows of the remainder of fruit across the top of the lettuce, alternating colors to create an attractive pattern. Sprinkle the raisins over the rows of fruit.

✤ Drizzle the French dressing over the entire platter including the cheese rounds. Serve immediately.

SERVES 4

Salade de Monte Carlo

¾ cup (177 ml) homemade mayonnaise
½ tsp. (2.5 ml) ground cinnamon
1 red grapefruit peeled and sectioned (membrane
  removed)
2 oranges peeled and sectioned (membrane
  removed)
1 cup (237 ml) diced celery
1 cup (237 ml) diced apple with skin
Seeds from one pomegranate
1 banana sliced into ¼ inch pieces (optional)
Lettuce leaves for serving (optional)

✤ Blend the cinnamon into the mayonnaise and set aside.

✤ Hold the grapefruit and oranges over a small bowl when sectioning to catch the juices. Place the sections in a large mixing bowl.

✤ Place the diced apple in the juice from the citrus fruit and coat the apple pieces entirely. (The citrus juices will prevent the apple from turning dark.)

✤ Add the celery and the pomegranate seeds to the large bowl of fruit.

✤ Lift the diced apple out of the juice with a slotted spoon and add to the fruit bowl.

✤ Just before serving gently fold in the banana (if using) and the seasoned mayonnaise and place scoops of the fruit on lettuce leaf cups.

✤ Alternately you can use the orange rind cups as your serving cups if you have cut the skin in a diamond pattern around the middle of the oranges when beginning. The recipe makes enough for four to six.

*Using banana is delicious but it must be sliced at the very last moment prior to serving as it will darken and become soft if prepared in advance. Placing the slices in the citrus juice will not be effective and the banana will become mushy.

Our photo shows a dish décor of sweet balsamic glaze, which was applied from a narrow nozzle squeeze bottle.

Salade King Edward

This salad is similar to what we call Waldorf salad in America and may be served in the manner you would normally serve Waldorf salad. However, this salad contains bananas and must be served immediately after completion.

> 3-4 cups (710-946 ml) assorted tender lettuce
> leaves
> 1 large red eating apple (Fuji, Gala, Red
> Delicious, etc.)
> 2 medium stalks of celery
> 2 fresh bananas
> 1 cup (237 ml) green grapes
> 1 cup (237 ml) red grapes
> ½ cup (118 ml) chopped walnuts

Dressing
> ¾ cup (177 ml) homemade mayonnaise
> 2 hardboiled egg yolks
> ½ tsp. (2.5 ml) fresh lemon juice
> 1 tsp. (5 ml) sherry wine

✤ Make the dressing by pushing the egg yolks through a sieve to finely pulverize them. Add to the mayonnaise. Add the lemon juice and the sherry wine and blend all well. Refrigerate until ready to assemble the salad.

✤ Cut the bananas in half and then into julienne strips about ¼ inch thick. Brush lightly with lemon juice.

✤ Cut the apple into thin wedges removing the core and brush lightly with fresh lemon juice.

✤ Cut the celery stalks into diagonal pieces about ½ inch long.

✤ In a large bowl lightly toss the lettuce in about half of the mayonnaise dressing. Place the lettuce on a large chilled serving platter.

✤ Arrange the fruit and celery in a circular pattern on the lettuce alternating the red and green grapes as the outer circle of fruit. Place the julienne of banana like spokes between the grapes.

✤ Drizzle the remaining mayonnaise dressing over the fruit. Sprinkle the chopped walnuts over the top. Serve immediately.

SERVES 4

Note: You may wish to toast the walnuts lightly to enhance the flavor and draw out the delicious walnut oil. Also you may wish to slice the majority of grapes in half except those you will use to garnish the top.

Salade Italienne Moderne

This is a delicious salad to serve as a full luncheon plate or in smaller portions as a side salad. Quantities given are for a luncheon size salad for four. Just reduce the quantities by at least half for side salads.

2 medium Yukon potatoes, boiled and chilled
4 medium ripe red tomatoes
8 thin slices of prosciutto
8 thin slices of smoked ham
16 thin rounds of pepperoni
6 cups (1420 ml) (approximately) of mixed greens
¼-⅓ cup (59-79 ml) of roughly chopped basil
  leaves
½ cup (118 ml) fine olive oil
2 Tbsp. (30 ml) red wine vinegar
2 small anchovies in oil
20 pitted black olives in brine
Salt and pepper to taste

❋ Mix the oil and the vinegar together, beating with a whisk until well incorporated. Mash the anchovies and whisk into the oil mixture until well blended into a smooth dressing. Taste and add pepper but the anchovy should bring enough salt flavor to the dressing. If not, add a small dash of salt.

❋ If needed, tear the lettuce into bite-size pieces, blending in the basil leaves and place on four chilled plates, dividing evenly.

❋ Slice the potato lengthwise into four slices and then julienne the slices thicker than matchsticks but not too heavy. Arrange on each salad in spokes, using one half of a potato on each plate.

❋ Cut the tomatoes into wedges and arrange them between the potato spokes around the plate.

❋ Cut the ham in thick julienne sticks as the potato and place in the spoke pattern, too.

❋ Roll the prosciutto into rolls from the short side and cut each roll on the diagonal. Place four cut rolls around each plate.

❋ Randomly place the pepperoni on top of each salad; four pieces per salad.

❋ Drizzle all the salads with the creamy dressing and top with olives. Serve immediately.

SERVES 4 AS A LUNCHEON PLATE

Note: Shaved slices of Parmesan are also a nice
  addition to this salad.

Salade du chef "Sophie"

SOPHIE'S CHEF SALAD

Once per month the local Café de la Tour offers "Fish & Chips" for the local British residents. If deep fried is not on your diet you may order the Chefs Choice Salad, which is the direction I take each month, while living in Les Arcs.

Approximately 2 full cups (437 ml) of assorted torn greens
1 hardboiled egg
1 medium tomato cut into wedges
½ cup (118 ml) Emmental cheese or Swiss cheese cut into dice bites
3 or 4 thin slices of red onion
5 thin slices of smoked salmon
4 small Red Mullet fillets sautéed in butter
1 Tbsp. (15 ml) capers
Lemon wedge

❁ Place the torn greens on a large chilled serving plate. Lay the salmon slices over the greens.

❁ Intersperse the Red Mullet fillets.

❁ Circle the plate with the egg and tomato

❁ Drizzle with French dressing and garnish with the lemon wedge for the guest to squeeze over the salad.

SERVES 1

Salade Astor

A very simple salad with complex flavor due to the chicory and watercress. Great as a side salad and a departure from the norm.

2 cups (473 ml) Escarole torn
1 cup (237 ml) chicory greens torn
2 cups (473 ml) watercress
1 seedless cucumber sliced very thin, skin left on
½ red sweet pepper, julienne thin
½ green sweet pepper, julienne thin
¾ cup (177 ml) homemade mayonnaise
¼ cup (59 ml) heavy cream or crème fraîche
Salt and pepper

❀ Gently toss the chicory, Escarole, and watercress together with the cucumbers in a large chilled salad bowl.

❀ Mix the mayonnaise with the cream to lighten and drizzle ½ cup (118 ml) over the greens. Gently toss to lightly coat. If more is needed add by the tablespoon but do not over dress the greens.

❀ Divide the greens between four chilled serving plates and top with the red and green peppers. Lightly sprinkle with salt and pepper. Serve immediately.

SERVES 4 GENEROUSLY

Les Arcs rooftop.

Salade Derby

You could certainly serve this as a Derby Day Luncheon Salad, but it is good anytime. It is very appropriate as a plate salad for lunch, with a crusty baguette followed by fresh fruit. The vegetables can be prepared in advance and refrigerated separately in covered containers and assembled at the last minute. The dressing can also be prepared in advance and refrigerated in a covered container.

2 cups (437 ml) of petite carrots or julienned
  carrot sticks, blanched for 3 minutes and chilled
2 cups (437 ml) of diced boiled Yukon potato,
  chilled
2 cups (437 ml) of haricot vert (thin French green
  beans) blanched for 3 minutes and cut in half,
  chilled
2 cups (437 ml) of dried sausage cut in into diced
  bites
Lettuce leaves for four plates

Dressing
1 small truffle finely chopped OR 1 tablespoon
  (15 ml) finely chopped porcini mushroom
4 gherkin pickles finely chopped
½ cup (118 ml) French dressing made with
  Balsamic vinegar
1 hard-boiled egg finely minced

❋ Prepare all the vegetables as indicated using salted water for blanching. Use a fresh pot of boiling water for each vegetable. Drain and chill well.

❋ Dice sausage and set aside.

❋ To the ½ cup of French dressing add the truffle or mushroom, pickle, and the hardboiled egg. Be sure all those ingredients are very finely chopped. This could be done in a food processor taking care not to puree each item. Blend well and taste for seasoning and adjust if necessary with salt and pepper. Refrigerate for ½ hour.

❋ In a large bowl place all the vegetables and sausage bites and gently toss together with the dressing.

❋ Place attractive lettuce leaves on the chilled serving plates and scoop the vegetable mélange onto the leaves of lettuce. Garnish with a few slices of hardboiled egg if desired and fresh chopped parsley. Serve immediately.

SERVES 4

Salade Terre et Mer

One of the very best salads served at Le Cabanon, that I often enjoyed, sitting on their petit patio in front of the restaurant or late at night by the fireplace is the Salade Terre et Mer. Patrick, the owner is gracious and accommodating to all special requests. The menu is typical Provençal and yet Nouvelle in some regards, offering a full menu complete to delicious desserts. The chef, Manon is a seasoned fellow and unassuming but exacting. Located not far from the Pharmacy at 20 place Edouard Soudani, Les Arcs.

3-4 cups (450 ml) Assorted Salad Greens
*1 cup (190 g) cooked medium salad shrimp, tails
  removed*
1 cup (225 g) diced cooked chicken breast
4 generous slices smoked salmon
*1 cup (2225 g) sautéed lardons or small diced
  thick bacon*
*1 cup (225 g) lightly sautéed baby scallops or
  large scallops cut in half (May be sautéed in the
  drippings of the lardons/bacon)*
½ (75 g) cup thinly sliced red onion
12 fresh tomato wedges (two fresh tomatoes)
*1 (125 g) cup roughly sliced or diced fresh
  mushrooms (Set aside 12 full slices)*
12 thin slices of cucumber with peel left on
12 triangles of fresh pineapple
4 lemon slices
Balsamic Glaze
Vinaigrette for 4 salads

❧ Place the assorted greens, blended with the onion, on four large plates. Lightly drizzle with the vinaigrette.

❧ Top each with the mixture of the shrimp, chicken, lardons and scallops. Drizzle more vinaigrette over the seafood and meat.

❧ On the very top place a slice of the smoked salmon.

❧ Around the plate edge place three pieces of each: pineapple wedges, sliced mushroom, cucumber and tomato wedges. Add one lemon slice to each plate.

❧ Garnish the cucumber with a ring of the balsamic glaze and possibly dots of the glaze between each garnish.

SERVES 4 AS A FULL LUNCHEON PLATE

In the Parage

Œufs divers a la Cocotte.

Duchess
farcie avec purée de champs. mele avez
farce de volaille mettere l'œuf couvert
de crème et cuit.

St Hubert
purée de gibier cordon fumet de gibier

— Aurore —
hard boiled, sliced in cream gratineed

Chanoinesse
Shrimps & Lobster truffle, in cocotte glace.

Axel devoted a number of pages to egg dishes and we have selected a few that should be attractive to many. Starting with an omelet that is Max's favorite, we note that an omelet, properly made, can be the star of any afternoon luncheon or late evening meal, not just breakfast.

On one of my very early trips to France turbulence was the norm for the major portion of the trip and by the time I arrived in Paris my stomach was begging to be relocated. My husband sought out a very lovely little restaurant and I reluctantly agreed to try to eat. I must have looked a bit green around the gills and suggested to the waiter that I needed something very mild to sooth my stomach. Bein! Exactomont! And I was served the best omelet I have ever had. It was light, moist and soothing and I was cured. Unfortunately, The Mule de Pape is no longer in business in Paris.

Never underestimate the value of a good omelet!

Omelette aux Cepes de Max

3 eggs beaten
4 or 5 cepes (mushrooms) sliced
1 Tbsp. (15 ml) olive oil
1 clove of garlic finely minced
2 slices of thick bacon diced and cooked crisp
2 tsp. (10 ml) chopped parsley
1 Tbsp. (15 ml) butter
Salt and pepper

❀ Fry the bacon until crispy but not hard. Drain off the fat and reserve the bacon.

❀ In the same skillet (preferably a nonstick skillet) heat the olive oil hot and sauté the mushrooms. When they begin to turn golden on the edges add the minced garlic and cook one minute longer. Remove and reserve.

❀ Wipe the skillet clean and melt the butter until it bubbles. Pour in the beaten egg. Using a rubber spatula begin to pull the sides up and away from the edges of the pan so the liquid egg can replace the cooked egg underneath.

❀ Continue until the egg has firmed up but is still moist and shiny. Do not cook dry.

❀ Scatter the mushroom, bacon and garlic onto the cooked egg. Season lightly with salt and pepper. Fold the omelet over onto itself and slide out of the pan onto a heated plate.

SERVES 1

Now for Max's sweet omelet!

Omelet Sucree

3 eggs separated
½ tsp. (2.5 ml) sugar
2 Tbsp. (30 ml) orange marmalade, room
   temperature
1 Tbsp. (15 ml) butter

❀ Beat the egg whites until light and fluffy, but not stiff.

❀ Beat the egg yolks until lemon color.

❀ Fold the whites into the yolks gently until well combined but not deflated.

❀ In a nonstick skillet melt the butter until foamy. Pour in the egg mixture. Using a rubber spatula begin to pull the sides up and away from the edges of the pan so the liquid egg can replace the cooked egg underneath. Continue until the egg mixture is set and puffy.

❀ Spread the orange marmalade onto the center of the omelet and fold over onto itself. Slide onto a heated serving plate and lightly sprinkle with the sugar. A dollop of marmalade on the side is a nice garnish.

Divers œufs Cocotte

VARIOUS TYPES OF EGGS IN COCOTTE

The term "Cocotte" refers to being baked in a casserole or small ramekin. Many French egg dishes are prepared in this manner and actually allows a hostess, serving a brunch or the family, to prepare the cocotte a bit in advance and bake individual ramekins all at once for last minute serving. As a departure from Eggs Benedict try one of these delicious dishes for your next lazy Sunday morning brunch.

Eggs Duchesse

¾ cup (177 ml) finely minced white mushrooms
½ medium onion finely minced
2 Tbsp. (30 ml) butter
1 tsp. (5 ml) dry thyme
1 cup (237 ml) fresh chicken livers
2 Tbsp. (30 ml) butter
2 Tbsp. (30 ml) heavy cream
1 garlic clove
Salt and pepper
4 fresh eggs
4 Tbsp. (59 ml) heavy cream

❋ Preheat oven to 350°F (180°C).

❋ Sautee the mushrooms and onions in the 2 tablespoons (30 ml) of butter until soft and well blended. Lightly season with salt and pepper and thyme.

❋ Divide this mixture between 4 lightly buttered individual (5 oz.) ramekins. Set aside.

❋ In the same skillet melt the next 2 tablespoons (30 ml) of butter until foamy. Rinse and drain well the chicken livers, patting them dry with paper towels and then finely chop.

❋ Finely mince the garlic clove and add to the livers. Sauté in the melted butter for 5 minutes

❋ Add the 2 tablespoons (30 ml) heavy cream. Season with salt and pepper. Cook for 2 more minutes until all is incorporated and the cream has been absorbed by the "liver pâté." Divide this mixture between the ramekins on top of the duxelle (mushroom) mixture.

❋ Carefully break an egg into each ramekin on top of the pâté mixture. Drizzle each egg with 1 tablespoon (15 ml) heavy cream and season with salt and pepper.

❋ Place the ramekins in a Bain Marie* having the water come up half way on the ramekins. Place in the hot oven and bake 8 to 10 minutes.

❋ You do not want the yolk to harden. Serve with toast points.

SERVES 4

Note: The pâté layer can also be a slice of Josephine's Pâté included under appetizers on page 20.

*Bain Marie refers to a pan of warm water into which you place the item you are baking. This will allow the casserole or ramekin ingredients to bake gently and with moisture.

Oeufs Aurore

6 peeled hard boiled eggs
1 cup (237 ml) grated Swiss cheese or Emmental
  cheese
4 Tbsp. (59 ml) butter, softened
4 Tbsp. (59 ml) heavy cream
Salt and pepper

Note: Max recommends that you may add finely chopped cooked shrimp or lobster under the cheese or even very thin slices of truffle should you be so lucky to have some on hand! This is also a recipe where you may use your imagination to add other ingredients and flavors.

❉ Preheat oven to 400°F (200°C).

❉ Butter 4 individual au gratin dishes (7 oz size) using 1 tablespoon (15 ml) butter per dish.

❉ Slice the eggs, getting about 6 slices per egg, or use an egg slicer. Place the egg slices overlapping in the au gratin dishes, about one and one half egg per dish. Season with salt and pepper.

❉ Sprinkle each dish with ¼ cup (59 ml) of the cheese and drizzle 1 tablespoon (15 ml) heavy cream over each au gratin dish.

❉ Place the au gratins on a flat baking sheet, and bake in the hot oven for 3 minutes. Turn the oven up to Broil and broil for 2 to 3 minutes, watching carefully that the cheese only lightly browns and melts.

❉ Serve immediately with toast points.

SERVES 4

Courtesy and copyright of Jacqui Brown from www.frenchvillagediaries.com.

Oeufs Suzette

In this recipe the baking dish is actually the outer skin of the baked potato, however setting each potato in an individual oval au gratin will allow ease for serving.

> 4 medium size Russet potatoes washed well
> 2 Tbsp. (30 ml) olive oil
> 2 Tbsp. (30 ml) sea salt or kosher salt
> 6 Tbsp. (89 ml) butter
> 6 to 8 medium cooked shrimp
> ⅓ cup (79 ml) heavy cream
> Salt and pepper
> 4 fresh eggs, lightly poached in advance
> ½ cup (118 ml) Mornay sauce

✤ Preheat oven to 350°F (180°C).

✤ Rub the potatoes with the olive oil and dust with the sea salt. Place on baking sheet and bake until, when pierced with a fork, they are completely tender to the center, about 35 minutes. Allow to cool to be able to handle them easily. Do not refrigerate.

✤ With the potato lying on its side, slice off a top portion of the skin to allow you to scoop out the potato, taking care not to tear the skin. You will want to allow about a ¼ of an inch of the potato to stay attached to the skin all around the inside.

✤ Place the scooped potato in a bowl.

✤ Heat the heavy cream and the butter in the microwave or in a small sauce pan, until the butter is completely melted.

✤ Add this mixture to the potatoes, mashing together until the potatoes are well blended. If the potatoes are too stiff, heat a little more cream and add in 1 tablespoon (15 ml) full between blending. Do not make too soft and runny. Mixture should be kept hot or very warm.

✤ Dice the cooked shrimp and add to the potato mixture and season with salt and pepper to taste.

✤ Place the mixture into the potato skins making an indentation in the top of the mixture to place the egg.

✤ Spoon the Mornay sauce evenly over the four stuffed potatoes. Sprinkle lightly with paprika for color.

✤ Place into a hot oven for 5 minutes and then turn up the broiler and broil for 2 minutes taking care not to burn the Mornay sauce. Serve immediately.

SERVES 4

Note: For the best and prettiest poached eggs, be sure the eggs are as fresh as possible. Add a tablespoon of white vinegar to the poaching water, which should only simmer, not boil. Always remove the eggs with a slotted spoon.

Poché's.

47

Œufs a la Dreux pochés froid sur salade de point d'asperges sauce chaufroid - a blanc de truffes gelée ou tour

Œufs Dufferin
sur crouton de Hominy frit. Sauce raifort Crème a l'anglaise

Œuf's Poché Thorndike
sur Muffin Anglaise Jambon grillé Sauce Crème et gratiné

Duchess
On toast, Madeira Sauce, truffles and asparagus..

Œuf's Georgette
In baked potato with Shrimps and Shrimp Sauce. gratine

" " Patti
on toast with broiled Ham, Tomato Sauce with fine herbs

" " Touraine
on artichoke, et glacé mornay.

" " Chartres
with fresh estragon Sauce Holandaise

" " Suzette
In baked potato, Shrimp Sauce.

" " Marie Louise
puree of Mushrooms, on Artichock botton & Cream Sauce.

Oeufs a la Anno

This delicious egg dish can be served as an opener to a more relaxed meal, for Sunday brunch or as a lovely main luncheon plate. The blend of distinct flavors will awaken any palate and the cook will be a star!

½ lb. (227 g) white mushrooms diced
3 Tbsp. (44 ml) unsalted butter
4 slices of toasted Brioche or toast points
1 cup (237 ml) crab claw meat, canned or cook
 fresh
1 cup (237 ml) white cream sauce (page 145)
1 Tbsp. (15 ml) tomato paste
8 poached eggs, very soft
1 Tbsp. (15 ml) finely chopped parsley
4 thin slices of truffle (optional)

✤ In a small skillet melt the butter until foamy. Add the diced mushrooms and sauté until tender about 3 minutes. Season with a dash of salt and pepper to taste. Set aside to cool to room temperature.

✤ Pick over the crab meat to be sure no shell is in the meat. Hold at room temperature.

✤ Warm the white cream sauce and add the tomato paste and blend well. Do not over heat or boil the cream sauce.

✤ Poach the eggs in simmering water with a tablespoon (15 ml) of white vinegar until whites are set and the top of the yolk is covered white; do not overcook the eggs. Remove and drain in paper towel.

✤ On a heated plate place the toasted bread and top with the mushroom mixture, dividing it evenly between the 4 plates.

✤ Top the mushroom mixture with the crab meat again dividing it evenly about ¼ cup (59 ml) per plate.

✤ Spoon ¼ cup (59 ml) of the cream sauce over the crab and top with the parsley. If using truffles, place the delicate slice on top of the sauce. Or julienne the truffle slices very thin and place on the top in a lattice pattern. Serve immediately with champagne. Voila!

SERVES 4

Oeufs Gourments

Place the poached eggs on top of slices of foie gras that are resting on toasted bread triangles or squares (crusts removed before toasting) and drizzle the top with warm Béarnaise sauce.

Note: Foie gras can be purchased in tins in any gourmet shop in various degrees of quality. I've never met a foie gras I did not like in any quality. My friend Kim, here in Provence, gave me a foie gras cutter and a tin of foie gras for Christmas. What a delightful gift. It's a marble base with a handle that is similar to a cheese cutter with a thin wire. Makes perfect cuts in any thickness desired.

Oeufs Sarah Bernhardt

✤ Using ripe sturdy tomatoes cut the top off the tomato and remove the seeds and interior pulp.

✤ Mix together fine dry bread crumbs with a little chili pepper or cayenne pepper and salt and pepper.

✤ Place a broken egg into the tomato cavity. Top with about 2 tablespoons (30 ml) of seasoned cream sauce and top the cream sauce with 2 tablespoons (30 ml) of bread crumbs.

✤ Bake in a preheated 375°F (190°C) oven for 10 minutes or until the tomato is tender but not losing its shape.

✤ Serve on a heated small plate with finely chopped parsley sprinkled around and a drizzle of Balsamic cream across the top.

Oeufs Sarah Bernhardt

$\mathcal{M}$eat in France is often unrivaled by other countries. The famous Limousin and Charolais beef; where the bull has been castrated, grazed on lush meadow grasses and fattened to go to market with tender marbling throughout the various cuts and aged for optimum tenderness, is well known and coveted by chefs and home cooks.

However there are many cuts of beef and there are hundreds of recipes for preparing all the cuts available. Axel dealt with mostly filets with exception of beef for Daubes. The French love Beouf because of the potential for so many staple dishes handed down for generations.

Veal was a favorite of Axel's and it appears on his menus and in the ledger numerous times. This tender meat of the calf is extremely popular in France and significantly in the northern regions, in spite of its costly nature. Max demonstrates for us his

technique with veal that is sure to please friends and family alike. In the veal arena we find sweetbreads, the thymus gland of veal and some very tasty ways to prepare these delicacies.

Think of France and most travelers will think of Sisteron lamb from the north of Provence. The major lamb recipe here is the *gigot*, or leg of lamb, roasted directly on a rack over potatoes. Filled with garlic, rosemary, anchovies and lardons, its flavor is unparalleled.

Poultry is a constant fall back for meat on the French table and duck is probably the king of French poultry along with small game birds. Axel offers a dish that is simple and hugely delicious; Poulet Sauté Crecy. And the Basquaise chicken is a dish to warm you and bring family and friends together in joyful dining.

Chicken Sauté Baillard
sauté a blanc garniture truffs, champignon
en juliene, croûtons de foie gras.

Chicken Sauté Chercy
Sauté a blanc garniture hinter a la
Villeroy croquette de pommes de terre.

Chicken Sauté Archiduc
sauté a blanc fini a la creme double
feuill d'estragon et lames de truffes

Chicken Sauté Argenteuille
sauté a blanc garniture pointe d'Asperg
et lames de truffes fleurons. - Portwin.

Poulet Sauté Chercy

1 2-3 lb. (907 g-kg 361 g) chicken cut into 8 pieces
  OR 4 legs and 4 thighs
2 Tbsp. (30 ml) unsalted butter
2 Tbsp. (30 ml) olive oil
½ cup (118 ml) heavy cream
½ cup (118 ml) Béchamel
4 medium carrots cut into dice (¼ inch pieces)
Salt and pepper
finely chopped parsley (optional)

❃ In a sauce pan boil the carrots in salted water until tender but not too soft. Drain and reserve keeping hot.

❃ Wash and completely dry the chicken pieces.

❃ In a deep heavy bottom skillet, melt the butter and add the olive oil and heat over medium high heat until frothy.

❃ Add the chicken and sauté until completely golden brown on all sides.

❃ Add the Béchamel and the cream and lower heat to a simmer. Simmer covered for 30 minutes.

❃ Add the drained carrots and simmer another 5 minutes. Taste for seasoning and make any adjustment with salt and pepper.

❃ Plate on a heated serving platter or individual plates, allowing 2 pieces per serving and dividing the carrots evenly between the plates or circling the chicken on the platter.

❃ Garnish with chopped parsley if desired.

SERVES 4

Low Calorie Version

❃ Using all the ingredients listed above, eliminate the cream and the Béchamel. Replace this with 1 cup (237 ml) of chicken stock and ½ cup (118 ml) dry white wine.

❃ Once the chicken has browned, add the stock and the wine and cover to simmer for 30 minutes.

❃ Add the carrots and 1 tablespoon (15 ml) finely chopped parsley and raise the heat to medium high and cook uncovered for 5 more minutes. The liquid will reduce by ½ and make a light sauce.

❃ Add salt and pepper to taste.

SERVES 4

Chicken Sauté Archiduc

4 chicken legs
4 chicken thighs
Salt and pepper
3 Tbsp. (44 ml) unsalted butter
⅓ cup (79 ml) Sherry or Port wine
⅓ cup (70 ml) heavy cream
1 Tbsp. (15 ml) finely chopped fresh tarragon
1 medium small truffle thinly sliced
Optional: Sliced white mushrooms and 1 Tbsp.
 (15 ml) white truffle oil (see below)

❧ Wash and completely dry the chicken pieces. Lightly salt and pepper them.

❧ In a large heavy bottom skillet melt the butter until foamy. Add the chicken pieces and sauté them for 5 minutes over medium heat, turning constantly and only allowing them to turn lightly golden, not brown.

❧ Lower heat if necessary to avoid browning. Remove the chicken from the skillet and set aside to keep warm.

❧ Raise the heat and deglaze the pan with the sherry or port wine, scraping up any bits that remain in the pan from the chicken.

❧ After the wine has reduced by half add the cream and simmer on low heat for 2 minutes.

❧ Add the fresh chopped tarragon and return the chicken to the skillet.

❧ Cover and allow to gently simmer over a low heat for 20 minutes or until a meat thermometer in the thickest part of the thigh registers 140°F (60°C).

❧ Add the truffles, if using, or substitute thinly sliced white mushrooms and blend gently into the remaining sauce. (If using mushrooms you may add 1 tablespoon (15 ml) of white truffle oil to the skillet when you add the cream.)

❧ Taste for seasoning and add salt and pepper if necessary.

❧ Plate individually on heated plates or on a platter and drizzle the pan sauce over all. Sprinkle with a bit more of the fresh chopped tarragon.

SERVES 4, TWO PIECES EACH

Guinea Hen Escoffier

Should you be able to purchase guinea hens then by all means use them. A Guinea hen is called a *Pintade* in Southern France and they weigh anywhere from one and one half pounds to three and one half pounds. We are suggesting using a Capon Hen if you cannot obtain a Guinea. Plan on at least one pound of a whole hen per person.

> *1 or 2 two lb. (454 kg) hens*
> *bacon strips – enough to fully wrap the hen(s)*
> *2 Tbsp. (30 ml) butter per hen*
> *2 Tbsp. (30 ml) olive oil*
> *¾ cup (177 ml) white wine*
> *2 Tbsp. (30 ml) tomato puree*
> *2 cups (473 ml) chicken stock*
> *½ cup (118 ml) diced fresh tomato*
> *2 tsp. (10 ml) paprika*
> *¾ cup (177 ml) fresh sliced white mushrooms or*
> * chanterelles*
> *Salt and pepper*

❀ Preheat oven to 375°F (190°C).

❀ Wash and dry the hen well then rub with the butter.

❀ Wrap the hen all around with the bacon strips and secure them overlapping on the back with small metal skewers or toothpicks. Butchers twine may also be used to tie the hen.

❀ In a deep lidded casserole or ovenproof kettle, bring the olive oil to a high temperature and sear the hen all over keeping the bacon wrapped as you turn the hen. Sear until the bacon begins to lightly brown, about 5 minutes.

❀ Add the white wine and bring to a boil for about 3 minutes to slightly reduce.

❀ Add the stock and the tomato puree and mix around the hen. Reduce over medium high heat for about 8 minutes.

❀ Add the paprika and the mushrooms, blending around the hen and basting the entire hen in the sauce in the bottom of the kettle.

❀ Cover and place in a preheated oven for 50 minutes (70 minutes for 2 hens). At 10 minute intervals (5 times), remove the kettle from the oven and baste with the sauce, re-cover, and return to the oven.

❀ Remove the hen from the kettle and carve into pieces and place on a heated platter.

❀ Meanwhile place the kettle on medium heat and reduce the sauce until slightly thickened and spoon over the hen pieces.

❀ Serve with spinach ravioli or buttered noodles with caraway seed.

SERVES 4

Basquaise Chicken

A warming and comforting dish that reflects the style of Basque countryside cooking. Serve this dish with steamed rice or tiny dumplings flavored with herbs. (Rice is the traditional side used to soak up the good juices of the chicken.) The chili pepper is essential to this dish but be sure to wear kitchen gloves when chopping and seeding the pepper and keep hands away from your face or you will suffer an intense burning sensation. You may substitute 2 teaspoons (10 ml) dried crushed chili peppers if fresh are not available.

1 stewing chicken cut into 8 pieces
2 Tbsp. (30 ml) olive oil
2 whole garlic cloves
1 tsp. (5 ml) each salt and pepper
½ cup (118 ml) flour
1 large onion chopped
1 sweet green pepper chopped
1 sweet red pepper chopped
1 large or 2 medium tomatoes, peeled, seeded and
  chopped
1 cup (237 ml) dry white wine
¾ cup (177 ml) diced ham (do not use lunch meat
  ham)
1 small fresh red chili pepper seeded and finely
  chopped
1 Tbsp. (15 ml) chopped fresh parsley

❋ Prepare the chicken by placing the flour and salt and pepper in a plastic bag and shake the chicken until lightly coated with the flour. Shake off excess.

❋ In a large heavy bottom kettle or casserole heat the olive oil and add the garlic cloves. On medium heat cook the garlic until lightly golden and remove the cloves; discard. Raise the heat to medium high and add the chicken, browning it on all sides about 8 minutes. Add the tomatoes, green and red pepper, wine, ham and chili pepper. Cover the kettle and simmer for 20 minutes over a low heat. Remove the cover and taste for seasoning and add a bit of salt if needed. Continue to simmer uncovered for 30 more minutes as the sauce reduces. Serve immediately or cool and refrigerate and slowly bring back to hot over a low heat. Serve with a side dish of hot steamed rice with some herbs such as thyme, oregano, or parsley.

SERVES 4

Canard avec Miel

Duck in Provence is like beer to St. Louis. It is served smoked, confit, braised, roasted, fried, and grilled just to name a few methods. This recipe is an amalgamation of two of the most used ingredients in Provence; duck breast and honey.

The Glaze
½ cup (118 ml) balsamic vinegar
½ cup (118 ml) honey
½ cup (118 ml) Calvados (apple brandy)
Pinch of cayenne pepper
Pinch of sea salt
⅓ cup (79 ml) olive oil

✤ Boil the balsamic vinegar to reduce it to ¼ cup (59 ml).

✤ Add the honey and the Calvados.

✤ Flame off the Calvados and add the cayenne and sea salt.

✤ Remove from heat and allow to cool for about 5 minutes.

✤ Pour into a deep mixing bowl and slowly drizzle in the oil while beating with a whisk to completely emulsify. Refrigerate.

For the duck breast
4 medium duck breasts with skin on
Salt and white pepper
1 Tbsp. (15 ml) olive oil

✤ Preheat the oven to 450°F (230°C).

✤ Score the skin of the duck breast on the diagonal making two "X" cuts, not cutting completely through to the meat. Season the breasts on both sides with salt and white pepper.

✤ Heat a black bottom (cast iron) skillet over medium high heat.

✤ Add the oil and heat well but do not allow to smoke.

✤ Place the duck breasts skin side down in the hot skillet and sauté until the skin turns golden brown and has released from the skillet bottom.

✤ Turn the breasts and sear on the bottom for about 1 minute.

✤ Brush the bottom with the glaze and turn top side up again. Brush the skin side with the glaze and turn again so the skin side is now down.

✤ Place in the hot oven for 7 to 8 minutes. Remove and place the breasts on a cutting board. Cover with foil.

✤ Put the remaining glaze in the cooking skillet and heat over medium heat, whisking up the bits on the bottom of the pan.

✤ Simmer for a few minutes to reduce slightly.

✤ On the diagonal, cut the breasts into about 5 slices and fan on the plate. Drizzle the hot glaze over the breasts. Great served with the Garlic mashers on page 101.

Chicken Cutlet Czarina

Axel named this recipe to honor the Czarina Alexandria of Russia. Or possibly it was named by Escoffier as it appears in his cookbooks also! In 1904 the Russian revolution was 10 years away and her death by the Bolsheviks in 1918 only 14 years away. Axel could not begin to realize that a world war and the end of the Russian nobility would happen in only a little more than a decade. Growing up in a country where the nobility was highly respected by the people, there had been a close relationship of both the Danish and the Russian royal families.

As there is fois gras in this recipe we recommend using the Josephine's Pâté on page 20, as a substitute. Fois Gras is available in the USA in cans in specialty shops. Additionally you could use thin sliced and sautéed Portobello mushrooms.

4 boneless, skinless chicken breasts, pounded to ¼
  inch thick
½ cup (118 ml) flour
Salt and pepper
2 Tbsp. (30 ml) unsalted butter
2 Tbsp. (30 ml) olive oil
4¼ inch thick fois gras slices
24 thin fresh asparagus stalks cleaned and lightly
  stripped of outer fiber
Juice of ½ lemon

✽ Place the flour and salt and pepper in a plastic bag and mix well. Place the chicken breasts, one at a time, in the bag and shake to coat with the flour. Shake off excess and set aside.

✽ Melt the butter and the olive oil in a large skillet and bring to a hot temperature but not smoking or browning.

✽ Sauté the breasts on each side for 4 minutes.

✽ Place in a 375°F (190°C) oven for 10 minutes.

✽ In the meantime bring about 2 cups of salted water to boil in a large clean skillet and place the asparagus in the boiling water for 5 minutes until just tender but not losing the bright green color. Do not overcook the asparagus.

✽ Drain and lightly butter and drizzle with fresh lemon juice, set aside and keep warm.

✽ Place the chicken breast on a heated plate and place the fois gras on top of the chicken and then the asparagus tented around the chicken breast. Allow any lemon butter mixture to drip over all.

SERVES 4, 6 ASPARAGUS PER PLATE

Chicken Dijonnaise

On the menu at The Eagle's Nest for eleven years and a favorite of many guests, the dish is easy to make and stands up to fancy company or a good Sunday afternoon dinner.

2 whole double lobes of chicken breast OR 4 whole
  breasts with first wing joint
2 Tbsp. (30 ml) olive oil
Salt and pepper
1 cup (237 ml) sliced white mushrooms
1 Tbsp. (15 ml) Dijon Mustard
⅔ cup (158 ml) heavy cream
1 Tbsp. (15 ml) fresh chopped parsley
Salt and pepper

✽ Preheat oven to 375°F (190°C).

✽ Wash and dry the chicken. If using the lobes, cut apart and then fillet them by cutting through each breast horizontally to create two filets from each lobe. (You will then have 8 filets of the breasts.)

✽ In a large heavy bottom skillet bring the olive oil to a hot simmer.

✽ Salt and pepper the chicken well and add to the hot oil. Sauté until golden brown all over, about 5 minutes.

✽ Place the skillet in the preheated oven and roast for 20 minutes for the lobes and 30 minutes for the whole breast.

✽ Remove from oven and place the chicken on a heated platter and cover with foil to maintain temperature.

✽ In the skillet add the mushrooms and just a small amount of oil if needed to sauté the mushrooms for 3 minutes.

✽ Add the Dijon mustard and the heavy cream and stir to blend well. Bring to a bubble boil for just 1 minute and season with salt and pepper to taste. Pour the cream mixture over the chicken breasts and garnish with finely chopped fresh parsley.

SERVES 4 WITH THE WHOLE BREAST
AND CAN SERVE 6 WITH THE FILLET LOBES

Carved panel door in the Parage.

Cotes de Agneau Maison d'or

Faite grille la cotelett un cotée, garnise le cotée grille
avez du foi gras apre couvert avez farce de volaille
garniture fon dé artichauts coupe en dee ☐

Cotes de Agneau Louis Philippe

cotelette farcie Soubise garnitur farce a qunelle mela
de truffe hachés eveloppe de crepinette et pane au be
sauté, demi glace

Cotes de Agneau Victor Hugo

Faite grille la cotelett un cotée, et farcis la cotelett
et decore avez langue et truffe haché garni de piment
vert en juliene sauté et tomate sauté.

B(sur bearnaisse farci aux Parford un lame de truffe et glace de Via

Cardinalice

farcies avec Duxelle croustade piment Roux et Ver

Lamb (Agneau)

Noisette d'Agneau Brillant Savarin

As much as a procedure for cooking this recipe refers to the presentation as well. It is beautiful as well as delicious and can be the centerpiece for a lovely dinner party.

2 lbs. (907 g) filet of lamb
Salt and white pepper
4 cups (946 ml) of mashed potatoes from Yukon
  potatoes
2 beaten eggs
3 large ripe tomatoes
1 large or two small eggplant
2 large shallots
2 Tbsp. (30 ml) olive oil

❊ Make your mashed potatoes using 4 large Yukon potatoes boiled in salted water, drained, and mashed well with some hot milk and butter to form a nice thick consistency.

❊ Add the beaten egg to the hot potatoes and blend very well. Taste for seasoning and add salt and pepper if needed. Set aside, cover and keep warm.

❊ Dice the tomatoes, removing the seeds and dice the egg plant into about ¼ inch squares. Chop the shallots to a medium mince.

❊ In a medium saucepan heat the olive oil and sear the shallots for 2 minutes.

❊ Add the egg plant and sauté all for another 3 minutes.

❊ Add the diced tomato, cover the pan and stew the vegetables for 5 minutes over medium heat. Add salt and pepper to taste.

❊ Grill the lamb until the temperature internally registers 135°F (57°C) on a meat thermometer. Remove from the grill and cover with foil for 5 minutes.

❊ Place the mashed potatoes in a large piping bag or make one from a large plastic bag, with a snipped corner. On heated oven-safe dinner plates, pipe the potatoes in a circle about 4 to 5 inches (10-12 cm) round.

❊ Slice the lamb into ½ inch (1.3 cm) thick medallions and place three on top of the potatoes.

❊ Spoon the stewed tomato mixture around the outside of the potatoes. Place under the broiler for just 1 minute to singe the edges of the potatoes and reheat the lamb.

❊ Garnish with rosemary sprigs or parsley and serve immediately.

SERVES 4

Dining room at Le Logis du Guetteur restaurant.

Cotes de Agneau Maison d'Or

This composed dish is an attractive and tasty "company" main course and requires foie gras or Josephine's Pâté as the crowning glory. A minced chicken and artichoke stuffing provide a lovely contrast of flavors and texture.

Stuffing
2 chicken breasts cut into small dice
6 artichoke bottoms cut into small dice
2 finely minced garlic cloves
1 white onion finely diced
2 Tbsp. (30 ml) finely chopped parsley
Salt and pepper
2 Tbsp. (30 ml) butter
4 crisp crostini, crushed (toasted thin baguette slices)

2 lbs. (907 g) lamb cutlets (½ lb (227 g) each) pounded to ¼ inch (.64 cm) thick
1 Tbsp. (15 ml) unsalted butter
4 slices of foie gras or Josephine's Pâté (page 20)
2 Tbsp. (30 ml) finely chopped parsley

❀ In a skillet melt the 2 tablespoons (30 ml) butter and sauté the diced chicken breast until golden brown about 5 minutes.

❀ Add the onion and garlic and sauté for 2 more minutes.

❀ Add the artichoke bottoms, crostini, and salt and pepper and gently stir together for 2 minutes over the medium heat. Set aside and keep warm.

❀ In a clean skillet add the 1 tablespoon (15 ml) butter and bring to froth over medium high heat.

❀ Add the cutlets, taking care not to crowd or add two at a time so they can sear and not braise.

❀ Sear for 2 minutes and turn to only lightly sear for 30 seconds to lightly color, keeping the cutlet medium rare. *Alternately these cutlets can be seasoned with salt and pepper and placed on a very hot, oiled grill for just 2 minutes and quickly turned to color. This eliminates the 1 tablespoon (15 ml) butter.*

❀ On heated plates place ¼ of the chicken artichoke mixture in the center. Top with the lamb cutlet allowing some stuffing to rim the cutlet. Top the cutlet with the foie gras or paté. Sprinkle with finely chopped parsley.

❀ Serve immediately.

SERVES 4

Provençal Style Leg of Lamb

This recipe is truly an old Provençal dish that most likely was done on a spit in front of the fireplace with the potatoes resting in a casserole under the lamb. My friends Jacky and Kim served this to me just before I left Les Arcs the last time and it confirmed to me that it definitely should be included in the book. Axel alludes to this method of preparation in his Cote de Agneau Bussy and included truffles. Jacky relates, in his charming French accent, that his mother and grandmother prepared the lamb in this manner. It is best to do this in a self-cleaning oven, but even if I did not have that convenience, it's so good that a session cleaning ones oven is a small price to pay! Definitely a dish for a crowd and a bit costly but worth every cent!

> 1 10-12 lb. (4 kg 536 g–5 kg 443 g) lamb leg with
>   shank intact
> 1 tin of anchovies in oil
> 8-10 finely minced garlic cloves
> 5 strips of smoked bacon
> Salt and pepper
> Big bunch of fresh rosemary and rosemary sticks
> 2 lbs. (907 g) small fingerling potatoes or Yukon's
>   cut into quarters

❀ Preheat oven to 400°F (200°C)

❀ Prepare the leg of lamb by carefully cutting the top fat layer free of the meat and fold it back, keeping it attached at the back side of the leg. Basically you are creating a large flap of the fat covering.

❀ Lay the flap back and season with salt and pepper. Rub the meat with the garlic. Lay the anchovies across the meat and then cover with the strips of bacon. Top this with many sprigs of the rosemary on stems.

❀ Fold the layer of fat over all, pulling it as tightly as possible. Using a thin paring knife, poke small holes in the edge of the fat flap and insert rosemary sticks to secure the flap to the meat. Toothpicks or small metal skewers may also be used.

❀ Using a very large casserole or baking pan that is bigger than the leg of lamb, place it on the lower rack of the oven with just a small amount of water to cover the bottom of the pan.

❀ Place the prepared leg of lamb directly on the top rack, with a pan directly under it in the oven. Adjust the pan to be sure it is directly below the lamb.

❀ Roast the lamb for 20 minutes at 400°F (200°C). The initial drippings will fall into the bottom pan and the water will evaporate.

❀ Lower the oven temperature to 325°F (170°C) and add the well washed and unpeeled potatoes to the lower pan. Sprinkle lightly with some sea salt. Roast for 40-50 minutes until a meat thermometer inserted into the thickest part of the leg registers 130°F (54°C) for medium rare. Do not over roast the lamb as it is most flavorful when served slightly pink throughout.

❀ Remove from oven when the desired temperature is reached and allow to sit.

❀ Cover (with a foil tent) for 15 minutes before carving to allow the internal juices to be absorbed into the meat.

❀ Remove the rosemary sprigs and carve into slices and serve on a heated platter surrounding the slices with the roasted potatoes. Garnish with fresh rosemary sprigs.

❀ The Pickled Onion Confit on page 24 is a nice side with this dish. Fresh grilled or steamed asparagus is a perfect vegetable to serve.

*SERVES AT LEAST 10 GENEROUSLY, WITH ENOUGH
LEFT ON THE BONE FOR A LAMB STEW THE NEXT DAY*

Ris de Veau d'Artois
Aritichocke and fresh mushrooms, cream sauce

"   "   " Bonne Femme
onions, potatoes, lardons, mushrooms sauce.
"   "   " Goddard
Mushrooms, truffles, olives, quenelles, Madeira Sa

"   "   " Christophe Colomb
in tomatoes, sauce Cheron

Ris de Veau Melba
Braisse, Point D'Asperge Pimentost farci de Verme
Sauce Supreme

"   "   "   Veronique

Veal

Axel offers many options for preparing veal. A delicious, tender meat, it is often overlooked by today's home cook. It is a bit more expensive than beef, but for a special occasion or just for two it can make a delightful meal entrée. Many of the recipes in the old book included artichokes in some form and they certainly do compliment veal. Here we present a few of our favorite veal dishes inspired by Axel's writings.

Cotes de Veau `a la Crème

VEAL CHOPS IN MUSHROOM CREAM

4 veal chops 1½ inch (4 cm) thick
2 Tbsp. (30 ml) unsalted butter
1 Tbsp. (15 ml) olive oil
1 cup (237 ml) sliced white mushrooms
½ cup (118 ml) veal or poultry stock
½ cup (118 ml) heavy cream
2 beaten egg yolks
2 Tbsp. (30 ml) Madeira wine
Salt and pepper

❋ Preheat the oven to 375°F (190°C).

❋ In a heavy bottom skillet, heat the butter and the olive oil over medium high heat.

❋ Sear the chops for 2 minutes on both sides.

❋ Place in the oven for 15 minutes.

❋ Remove from the oven and place the chops on the serving platter and tent with foil to keep hot.

❋ In the skillet put the mushrooms over medium high heat and add a bit more olive oil (½ tablespoon or 7.5 ml) and quickly sauté in the drippings of the chops.

❋ Add the stock and scrape up any bits of brown from roasting the chops.

❋ Mix together the cream and the eggs and the Madeira wine and blend well. Slowly pour this mixture into the skillet with the mushrooms and stock.

❋ Simmer slowly while stirring, until the sauce begins to thicken and reduce. Do not boil or the sauce will separate.

❋ Add the salt and pepper to taste.

❋ Pour the sauce over the chops and garnish with chopped chervil or parsley. Serve immediately.

SERVES 4

Cote de Veau Marquise

VEAL CUTLETS WITH ARTICHOKE BOTTOMS AND MUSHROOM CREAM

4 veal cutlets
8 artichoke bottoms, canned in water or fresh
⅓ cup (79 ml) dried fine bread crumbs
1 tsp. (5 ml) dried thyme leaves
Salt and pepper
2 Tbsp. (30 ml) unsalted butter
1 Tbsp. (15 ml) olive oil
¾ cup (177 ml) finely chopped white button
  mushrooms
1 medium shallot finely minced
2 Tbsp. (30 ml) unsalted butter
½ cup (118 ml) heavy cream

❋ Pound the cutlets thin between plastic wrap.

❋ Place the artichoke bottoms in a food processor and mince finely with the thyme and bread crumbs. Season lightly with salt and pepper.

❋ Place a spoonful of the mixture across the bottom edge of each cutlet and roll the cutlet to form a roll. Fasten with a toothpick.

❋ In a heavy bottomed skillet heat 2 tablespoons of butter and olive oil then sear the stuffed cutlets completely for about 4 to 5 minutes over medium high heat, gently rolling them back and forth to sear all around. Take care not to burn or over sear.

❋ Remove the stuffed cutlets to an ovenproof casserole and tent with foil to keep hot. In the same food processor bowl, process the mushrooms and the shallot until almost a puree.

❋ In the same skillet, melt the second 2 tablespoons (30 ml) butter and add the puree of shallots and mushrooms. Stirring constantly cook over medium high heat the mixture for 4 minutes.

❋ Add the cream and salt and pepper to taste, stirring constantly. Pour this mixture over the veal rolls and replace the foil and bake in a 350°F (180°C) oven for 20 minutes.

❋ With tongs lift out the veal rolls and remove the toothpicks and slice the veal rolls into three sections each, which will look like jelly roll slices.

❋ Return the slices to the casserole and spoon the sauce over them. Serve immediately.

SERVES 4

Veal Picatta

8 veal escalopes (2 per person)
½ cup (118 ml) flour
½ cup (118 ml) very fine dried bread crumbs
Salt and pepper
3 Tbsp. (44 ml) unsalted butter
1 Tbsp. (15 ml) olive oil
⅓ cup (79 ml) dry white wine
¼ cup (59 ml) fresh lemon juice
2 Tbsp. (30 ml) capers
3 Tbsp. (44 ml) soft butter (room temperature)

❋ Pound the veal escalopes thin between plastic wrap.

❋ Mix together the flour, bread crumbs, thyme, salt and pepper.

❋ Dredge the cutlets in the mixture, shaking off excess.

❋ Heat the butter and oil in a heavy bottom large skillet. When the butter and oil are hot but not browning add the cutlets. Sear on both sides about 2 minutes until golden brown.

❋ Add the wine and lemon juice and capers and bring to a quick boil, turning the cutlets once in the sauce that forms.

❋ Remove from heat and remove the cutlets from the skillet to a warmed serving platter.

❋ Add the butter to the skillet sauce in pieces and stir gently into the sauce. Adjust seasonings if needed. The sauce should thicken slightly.

❋ Pour over the cutlets. Top each cutlet with a thin slice of lemon and serve immediately.

SERVES 4

Sweetbreads

This tender, sweet meat is actually the thymus gland of the veal, or calf. Commonly referred to as Ris de Veal in French recipes, it is a well-loved dish all over France and particularly in Provence. Prepared correctly, it is a true gourmet dish that you will come to relish in your repertory of special dishes. A very good butcher will provide this meat for you, as it seldom is available in the local grocery store outside of European stores. Quality is very important here and a good butcher will know that and provide you with the best. Read through the recipes and follow all the instructions closely and you will be rewarded with a culinary delight.

At the market

To Prepare the Sweetbreads for any recipe

Soak the sweetbreads in cold water for at least two hours. Drain and rinse. In a large saucepan place the following ingredients:

5 cups (1183 ml) cold water
2 Tbsp. (30 ml) red wine vinegar
1 bay leaf
2 ribs of celery cut into thirds
½ chopped onion

2 medium carrots roughly cut
2 tsp. (10 ml) salt
2 lbs. (907 g) sweetbreads

❋ Bring all ingredients to a boil and simmer 10 minutes.

❋ Drain, discard all the vegetables and rinse the sweetbreads well. Remove any white membrane or ducts from the breads.

❋ Place on a flat plate and press them between another plate weighted down with can goods or a brick. Chill well. Refrigerate until ready to prepare as a main dish. Will hold, covered, in the refrigerator for 24 hours, thus this step can be accomplished in advance of the final dish preparation.

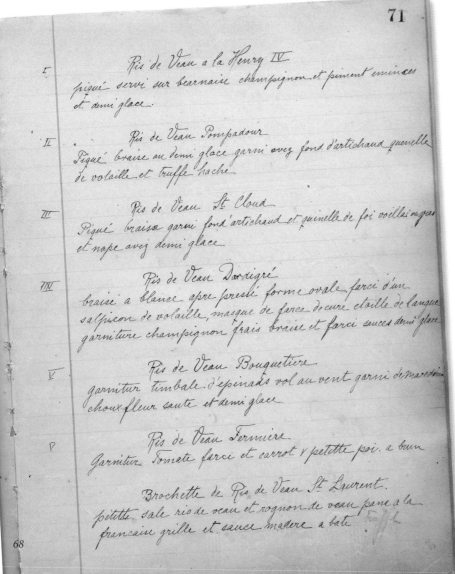

Ris de Veau Bonne Femme

Note: This recipe is translated as "the maid" and originates from the rural areas of France thus the potatoes and bacon side dish. It is a hearty winter plate to be served with crusty bread and a nice crisp green salad. A Bandol Rosé wine would be lovely with this dish.

2 lbs. (907 g) or 2 pairs sweetbreads, prepared as above
2 medium white or yellow onions, roughly chopped
4 medium Yukon potatoes
½ lb. (227 g) thick bacon, diced
5 Tbsp. (74 ml) unsalted butter (reserve 3 Tbsp. [44 ml])
2 Tbsp. (30 ml) olive oil
1 cup (237 ml) chopped white mushrooms
2 garlic cloves minced
½ cup (118 ml) veal or chicken stock
Salt and pepper
1 cup (237 ml) heavy cream or whipping cream

❋ Dice potatoes into about ½ inch squares and blanch in boiling salted water until tender but not soggy or overcooked, about 3 minutes. Drain well.

❋ In a large skillet sauté the bacon until lightly crisp. Drain most of the grease.

❋ Add the 2 tablespoons (30 ml) butter and the 2 tablespoons (30 ml) olive oil. Bring to a bubbly foam and add the onion and garlic and sauté for 2 minutes until the onion is almost transparent.

❋ Add the potatoes and sauté all about 8 minutes over medium heat not stirring too much so as to not mash the potatoes into the onion and bacon. Remove from the heat and add salt and pepper to taste, cover and keep hot.

❋ In a separate skillet melt the remaining 3 tablespoons (44 ml) of butter until foamy and sauté the sliced sweetbreads (cut on the diagonal about ¾ inch thick) until lightly browned.

❋ Add the mushrooms and sauté with the sweetbreads 2 minutes.

❋ Add the stock and reduce over medium heat for 4 to 5 minutes. Add the cream and simmer another 3 to 4 minutes until thick and creamy. Add salt and pepper to taste.

❋ On individual heated serving plates, place the potato mixture on the side and place the sweetbreads next to the potatoes and spoon the sauce from the pan over the sweetbreads.

SERVES 4

Ris de Veau aux Cepes

MAX'S SWEETBREAD RECIPE!

There are three basic steps to this recipe. Preparing the sweetbreads and sautéing and flaming them to create a sauce, preparing a simple polenta as a bed for the sweetbreads, and sautéing the vegetables as a garnish to the dish. You may prepare the sweetbreads and also sauté the vegetables a day in advance and hold them, covered, in the refrigerator to be reheated just before plating.

2 lbs. (907 g) or 2 pair sweetbreads, prepared as
  above
1 cup (237 ml) fresh cepe mushrooms
2 Tbsp. (30 ml) unsalted butter
½ cup (118 ml) warm brandy or cognac
¾ cup (177 ml) dry red wine
1 cup (237 ml) dry polenta
1 cup (237 ml) milk
1 cup (237 ml) water
1 tsp. (5 ml) salt
1 Tbsp. (15 ml) olive oil
½ cup (118 ml) fresh grated cow's cheese
1 cup (237 ml) small diced carrot
1 cup (237 ml) small diced celery
2 Tbsp. (30 ml) truffle oil or unsalted butter
Salt and pepper

❋ In a deep skillet, heat the 2 tablespoons (39 ml) of butter until frothy and sear the sweetbreads until lightly golden brown. Add the cepes and sauté for 1 minute.

❋ Warm the brandy and flambé it in the skillet. When the flame has died out add the red wine and simmer to reduce the liquid by one half.

❋ Prepare the polenta using the milk, water, and olive oil, which you have brought to a boil.

❋ SLOWLY add the polenta whisking continually to avoid lumps. Once all the liquid has been added, continue stirring over low heat for 4 minutes to completely cook the grain.

❋ Add the shredded cow's cheese and fold in completely. Float a dab of butter on the top and cover to keep hot until ready to plate.

❋ In a medium skillet, sauté the celery and carrots in the truffle oil until soft and translucent, about 4 to 5 minutes. Do not overcook.

❋ Place a large spoonful of the polenta in the center of a heated plate. Spoon ¼ of the sweetbreads into the center of the polenta.

❋ Spoon ¼ of the sautéed vegetables around the edge of the polenta. Drizzle the pan juice from the sweetbreads evenly over the top of the sweetbreads and the cepes.

SERVES 4

Ris de Veau Artois

2 pairs or 2 lbs (907 g) prepared sweetbreads
1 cup (237 ml) fresh artichoke hearts
3 cups (710 ml) cold water
Juice of 1 lemon
½ lb. (227 g) fresh white mushrooms cut into
  quarters
5 Tbsp. (74 ml) unsalted butter
½ cup (118 ml) veal or chicken stock (veal is best)
½ cup (118 ml) heavy cream or whipping cream
Salt and pepper to taste

❋ In a medium saucepan place the water, lemon juice, and artichoke hearts and cook until just tender to the fork, about 8 to 10 minutes once the water has come to a boil. Drain and pat very dry.

❋ Melt 2 tablespoons (30 ml) of the butter in a large skillet until foamy. Add the artichoke hearts and the mushrooms and sauté for 3 minutes.

❋ Add the stock and simmer until the stock is reduced by half. Add the cream and simmer gently 3 to 4 more minutes. Add salt and pepper to taste.

❋ Slice the sweetbreads on the diagonal about 3/4 inch (2 cm) thick. In another skillet bring the remaining 3 tablespoons (44 ml) of butter to a bubbling froth and sauté the sweetbreads until lightly brown over medium high heat. Do not overcook.

❋ Serve on a heated platter or four individual plates, with the hot artichoke mushroom sauce on top. Garnish with finely chopped parsley if desired.

SERVES 4

Tournedos à l'Aiglon.
Sauté servis sur croquette de pomme plate (Dauphine)
avec langue hashé dans la croquette, garniture financière
sur tournedos une croquette de foi gras avec une tiche de truf
(en form de poix)

Martin
Piment dous et cêpes 2 bouquets sauce brune et
pommes Parisienne.

Nicoise.
Tomate sauté fresh et Haricot vert.

Filet Mignon Dickerson
Champignon frais piment rouges tomate sauté
et chow chow pomme parisienne.

Esc   auce
per

Sur   gne, sauté
coupé   e Champignon
sauc

Sur   truffes et
Chau   St Tanige

Filet Rossini

There is controversy as to whether Axel was referring to a pork filet or a beef filet, so we allow you, the cook, to make that decision. In the late 1800's and early 1900's "filet' did refer to beef. Today a filet in France is considered pork. This recipe would be delicious with either!

4 1½ inch (4 cm) thick filet mignon steaks or pork
  steaks from the filet
Salt and pepper
1 Tbsp. (15 ml) olive oil
½ cup (118 ml) Madeira wine
1 Tbsp. (15 ml) white truffle oil
½ cup (118 ml) demi-glace or thick beef stock
1 Tbsp. (15 ml) butter
4 slices fois gras or Josephine's Pâté (page 20)
4 thin slices of truffle OR 8 thin slices of Portobello
  mushroom

❋ Completely dry and salt and pepper the steaks.

❋ Heat the olive oil in a heavy bottom skillet until it is almost smoking, over medium high heat. Sear on both sides for 3 to 4 minutes each side.

❋ Remove from the skillet to a heated serving platter and cover with foil.

❋ If using the mushrooms, sauté them in the skillet at this point and then place on top of the steaks and recover.

❋ If using the fois gras, sauté gently for 1 minute on each side in the skillet and place on top of the steaks. (If using the paté do not sauté, just serve at room temperature on the steaks.)

❋ Deglaze the skillet with the Madeira wine and then add the truffle oil and the demi-glace or stock.

❋ Reduce over medium heat until only about ½ cup remains.

❋ Remove from the heat and add the butter and swirl to melt and thicken the sauce.

❋ Pour the sauce over the steaks and garnish with the truffle slices if using. Serve on heated plates.

SERVES 4

Steak Béarnaise

Preparing Steak Béarnaise is very easy and so delicious your guests will marvel at your culinary skill. On page 146 is our recipe for Béarnaise sauce. You can prepare this a day or two in advance and refrigerate. Bring to room temperature before topping the steaks.

4 1½ inch (11 cm) thick Choice Rib Eye Steaks
* OR 1½ inch thick Filet Mignon steaks*
1 Tbsp. (15 ml) olive oil
1 Tbsp. (15 ml) unsalted butter
Salt and pepper
1 cup (237 ml) homemade Béarnaise sauce
4 sprigs fresh tarragon

❋ Salt and pepper the steaks and allow to sit out at room temperature for 30 minutes.

❋ In a large heavy bottom skillet, heat the oil and the butter until ALMOST smoking.

❋ Sear the steaks on each side 3 to 4 minutes per side.

❋ Remove the steaks from the skillet and place on a heated platter and cover tightly with foil for at least 5 minutes but not more than 8 minutes. The steaks will continue to cook themselves if left too long, but this process retains all the good natural juice of the meat.

❋ Plate individually on heated dinner plates and top with the warmed Béarnaise Sauce and garnish with a tarragon sprig.

SERVES 4

St. Roseline Winery & Convent

Chateau Sainte Roseline

Steak au Poivre

The secret to a great Steak au Poivre is using freshly ground black peppercorns. Avoid using the fancy mixtures and green peppercorns. If you have mortar and pestle it is the best way to open up the flavor of the peppercorns, otherwise use the coarsest setting on your pepper grinder. Additionally, the quality of the steak is critical and you should always use aged beef. A good butcher can cut these exactly as you request for uniform presentation.

*4 1lb. (454 g) choice New York Strip steaks about
  1½ to 2 inches (4 cm) thick*
⅓ cup (79 ml) coarse ground black peppercorns
5 Tbsp. (74 ml) unsalted butter
3 Tbsp. (44 ml) extra virgin olive oil
4-5 medium French shallots finely chopped
¼ cup (59 ml) brandy or Cognac
½ (118 ml) cup heavy cream
2 tsp. (10 ml) Dijon or coarse ground mustard

❧ Lay the steaks on the counter and sprinkle the peppercorns over all, pressing the pepper into the meat. Flip over and repeat on the other side. If you need more pepper, grind coarsely again. Allow the steaks to sit out on the counter or on flat cookie sheets for about 45 minutes at room temperature to absorb the flavor of the pepper.

❧ In a very large skillet bring the butter and the olive oil to a hot froth over medium high heat. Do not crowd the steaks or they will not sear correctly. You may wish to use two skillets with just two steaks per skillet.

❧ Place the steaks in the hot butter/oil mixture and sear on each side for about 3 to 4 minutes per side. If you like well done beef this is not a dish that you should be preparing as Steak Poivre should be served medium rare (about 130°F [54°C] in the center if using a meat thermometer).

❧ Remove the steaks from the skillet and place on a heated platter and cover to keep warm.

❧ Add the chopped shallots to the skillet and add a bit more butter if needed to sauté them for about 3 to 4 minutes until softened.

❧ Return the steaks to the skillet(s). Turn off the heat and add the brandy to heat it enough to flame. The heat from the skillet should be sufficient to warm the brandy.

❧ Light the brandy with a kitchen match or lighter and allow to flame until the flame dies out completely. (Take great care when flaming any liquors in a dish that you stand back to avoid flames catching your apron, hair or eyebrows!)

❧ Add the cream and the mustard and continue to cook over medium heat for about two minutes to thicken the sauce. Taste for seasoning and add salt if needed. Do not add additional pepper at this time. Plate individually onto heated dinner plates, spooning the sauce over the filet.

SERVES 4 GENEROUSLY

2000 year old Roman bridge

Beef Daube

This traditional Provençal dish is truly a reflection of the region, yet is now duplicated all over France. There are a number of variations and the dish is also made with sanglier, lamb or pork. Allow plenty of time to prepare this dish as it is better the longer it simmers as well as marinating in the first step. Use a cast iron kettle with a heavy lid if at all possible, such as a large Le Creuset Doufeu Oven.

2½ lbs. (907 g) beef chuck roast or shoulder meat,
*   cut into 1 inch (2.5 cm) chunks*
1 bottle dry red wine, Bordeaux or Pinot Noir
3 garlic cloves lightly crushed
1 large carrot cut into medium dice
1 large white or yellow onion cut into large
*   chunks*
1 celery stalk cut into medium dice
2 whole cloves
2 dried bay leaves
3 slices of orange with rind
1 tsp. (5 ml) each salt and pepper

Blend all the ingredients in a large glass bowl or non-reactive kettle and add the chunks of the beef. Cover and marinate overnight in a cool location, or in the refrigerator.

2 Tbsp. (30 ml) olive oil
¾ cup (177 ml) thick bacon diced
2 or 3 pork spare ribs (in lieu of the traditional
*   pig's foot)*
1 bouquet garni

2 cups (473 ml) beef stock
2 Tbsp. (30 ml) fresh orange zest

❋ Drain the beef from the marinade, reserving all the marinade. Blot the meat dry with toweling.

❋ In the large cast iron kettle or Le Creuset Doufeu Oven sear the diced bacon in the olive oil for 4 minutes, over medium high heat. Brown the meat in the kettle, preferably in two or three batches to avoid crowding and creating a braising effect.

❋ Add a bit more oil if needed between batches. Sear the individual ribs for 4 minutes. Set all the meat aside on a plate.

❋ Strain the marinade and add the vegetables to the hot kettle and stir to brown lightly.

❋ Add the marinade liquid to the kettle.

❋ Add the beef stock and the bouquet garni and the orange zest. Return the meat to the kettle.

❋ Bring to a boil and reduce to a very low simmer. Cover and simmer for at least 2 hours or until the beef is very tender.

❋ Remove the lid, taste for seasoning and add a bit of salt if needed and continue to simmer 30 minutes to reduce the liquid and thicken to a glaze consistency.

❋ Remove the rib bones and the bouquet garni and break up any of the rib meat into small pieces.

❋ Serve with small Yukon potatoes or a creamy polenta, or buttered noodles.

SERVES 6

Axel's books and cutlery.

Fruit de Mer
Seafood

A xel had a number of seafood dishes in his book and, in particular, lobster dishes. We have selected a few we think are relevant to today's cooking, although not necessarily low fat. However, for special occasions these lobster dishes are perfect.

Pomme du Terre et Pate
Potatoes & Pasta

Because Louis XVI latched onto potatoes as a means to relieve a famine in the latter 17th century, potatoes have become a staple on the French table. In the market today potatoes come in an amazing range of sizes and colors, and the French have recipes for them all. Axel offered numerous versions, of which we have selected a few for your enjoyment.

Garlic Mashers

Lots of French restaurants serve a quenelle of mashed potatoes, which is nothing more than forming the potatoes into a quenelle using two large serving spoons and placing the potatoes next to a meat or fish entrée on the serving plate. While a simple dish, these potatoes are full of flavor and make a nice accompaniment to almost any main meat or seafood dish. Also I might mention that in France, especially Provence, milk is eliminated and olive oil substituted. These will be slightly thicker or dryer than those with milk, but the flavor is excellent!

2 lbs. (907 g) Yukon potatoes scrubbed well, skins on
3 qts. (2839 ml) chicken stock or bullion
¼ lb. (113 g) (1 stick) butter
5 garlic cloves minced
Salt and pepper
1 cup (237 ml) whole milk or half & half
½ cup (118 ml) reserved cooking liquid

❋ Scrub and remove any eyes or dark spots from the potatoes.

❋ Cut the potatoes in small chunks. Put the potatoes in the stock and bring to a boil and cook until tender but not mushy. Drain well reserving ½ cup of the cooking liquid.

❋ While the potatoes are cooking, melt the butter in a sauce pan and add the garlic and cook over medium heat until the garlic is tender but not brown.

❋ To the drained potatoes add the garlic butter mixture and mash well. Heat the milk and add to the potatoes as you are mashing, a little at a time.

❋ Add salt and pepper to taste. If the potatoes are too stiff use a bit of the cooking liquid, up to ½ cup (118 ml). Be careful not to make the potatoes too

runny or you will not be able to form a quenelle. Do not worry about small lumps and do not use an electric mixer on the potatoes or they will turn to elastic strings.

❋ Using two metal serving spoons, dip them into very hot water and from the side of the spoon scoop out a full spoonful of the potatoes. Using the second spoon, roll the inside of the spoon over the top of the potatoes to make an oval egg-shaped form. Slide potato off the spoon onto a heated serving plate next to an entrée.

❋ Serve immediately.

MAKES ABOUT 16 QUENELLES

Other ways with potatoes

- Fingerling potatoes boiled in chicken stock and served whole with a dusting of chopped parsley.
- Sliced potatoes fried in duck fat until crispy.
- Cut potatoes into large slices and bake under a meat dish with carrots and leeks.
- Cook in fish stock with onions and serve in the stock with chunks of white boiled fish.
- Served as a diced "hash" with onions, garlic, celery and carrots; all pre-cooked, diced, and sautéed in olive oil with salt and pepper.
- Boiled and sliced and served cold in salads with tuna or herring.

Potato Cheese Gratin

This is an easy dish but it is necessary to be sure the potatoes have been squeezed of any moisture. Using a kitchen dish towel is the perfect way to wring out moisture.

3 Tbsp. (44 ml) butter
2 lbs. (907 g) Yukon or Idaho Potatoes
  scrubbed clean
½ cup (118 ml) heavy cream
3 medium eggs well beaten
½ cup (118 ml) grated Gruyère Cheese
Salt and pepper

❀ Preheat the oven to 400°F (200°C).

❀ Melt the butter and pour it into the casserole or baking dish you intend to serve in.

❀ Grate the potatoes, leaving on the skins. Squeeze out moisture in a tea towel and be sure they are as dry as possible.

❀ In a big mixing bowl, place the potatoes, cream, eggs, and cheese. Add salt and pepper to taste.

❀ Mix completely and pour into the baking casserole.

❀ Bake uncovered for 45 to 50 minutes until the top begins to crisp and become golden brown. Serve immediately.

SERVES 4 TO 6

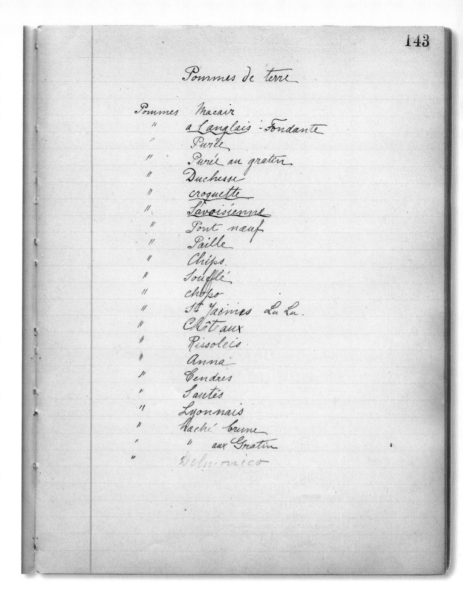

Pommes Anna

This old traditional dish was first served to me in a little back street Bistro in Avignon and it was simply delicious in its simplicity. Your oven must be very hot and preheated so the top crisps correctly, which becomes the bottom "crust."

2 lbs. (907 g) Idaho or Yukon potatoes, peeled
⅔ cup (158 ml) clarified butter
Salt and pepper

❀ Preheat oven to 400°F (200°C).

❀ Use a glass or heavy metal pie tin or round cake pan and drizzle 2 tablespoons (30 ml) of the clarified butter in the bottom.

❀ Using a mandolin, slice the potatoes very thin. Lay them on a dry tea towel and blot as dry as possible.

❀ Spiral the potatoes into the bottom of the pan in concentric circles, slightly overlapping each slice.

❀ Drizzle 2 tablespoons (30 ml) butter over this layer and lightly sprinkle with salt and pepper. Repeat this layering and butter until all is used, ending with a drizzle of butter.

❀ Place in the oven and bake for 1 hour until the top is crispy and golden brown.

❀ Remove from the oven and allow to cool just slightly to set. Invert onto a heated serving plate.

❀ Cut into pie slices to serve.

SERVES 4 TO 6

Pommes Anna

Pasta with Spinach & Lardons

*3-4 cups purchased fresh cheese tortellini or
  ravioli
1 cup (237 ml) lardons or thick bacon diced
3 garlic cloves minced
3 cups (710 ml) fresh spinach
½ cup (118 ml) toasted walnut pieces
1cup (160 ml) chicken stock
1 cup shredded Parmesan cheese*

❀ In a large sauté pan cook the lardons until beginning
to color.

❀ Add the garlic and cook for 2 more minutes.

❀ Add the olive oil and heat all through for 2 minutes.
Add the spinach and toss until wilted, 1 minute only.

❀ In boiling salted water cook the pasta until tender
about 4 to 5 minutes. Drain and reserve 1 cup (237 ml)
of pasta water, if using bullion make the stock in the
pasta water.

❀ Add the stock to the lardons and spinach pan and
add the cooked hot pasta.

❀ Add salt and pepper. Add the walnuts and gently
toss all together. Serve with shredded Parmesan cheese
on top. Serve immediately.

SERVES 4

Gnocchi de Pomme de Terre

Many people think of Gnocchi as an Italian dish, and it surely is served in abundance in Italy, although the word actually has its roots in old Provençal language; "inhocs." Served as a first course in small portions or as a main dish, these delicate little "dumplings" are the perfect carrier for various sauces and toppings. I personally love them in brown sage butter with a dash of Parmesan, but topped with pesto, tomato sauce, liver sauce or an herb sauce they are equally delicious. Some people boil them and place them in a buttered casserole with a light Mornay sauce on top and place under the broiler for a few minutes to brown on top. In Provence I have seen them served with a Beef Daube to soak up the juices. Magnificent!

2 lbs. (1 kg) waxy style potatoes, or bakers, peeled and cut up into chunks.
Salted water in large pan
½ tsp. (2.5 ml) freshly grated nutmeg
2 egg yolks
1 ¾ cup (414 ml) flour
1 Tbsp. (15 ml) olive oil
½ stick unsalted butter melted
Salt and pepper to taste
½ cup (118 ml) fresh grated Parmesan cheese

❋ In the boiling salted water place the potatoes and boil until they are tender, about 20-25 minutes, taking care not to overcook them.

❋ Drain them well and return them to the cooking pan and dry out over a medium heat for just a few minutes. Do not scorch them.

❋ Put the potatoes through a food mill or fine ricer into a large mixing bowl.

❋ Season with salt and pepper and nutmeg.

❋ Add the egg yolks and using a wooden spoon work the eggs into the potatoes.

❋ Work in the flour a bit at a time to give the dough a firm but not stiff texture. Continue until the dough is smooth. You may not use all the flour or need to add a bit more, depending on the moisture left in the potatoes and the size of the egg yolks.

❋ With well-floured hands, on a floured surface, roll out dough in long ropes about ½-¾ inch (1-2 cm) thick. Cut the ropes into 1-inch (2.5 cm) pieces.

❋ Using a fork dipped in flour roll it across the gnocchi on one side to create little groves. Do not flatten the gnocchi.

❋ In a large kettle of boiling salted water, add the olive oil and the gnocchi, dropping in only a handful at a time to avoid them sticking together. When they rise to the top continue to cook for 1 minute. Remove very gently with a slotted spoon to a buttered serving dish. Repeat until all the gnocchi are cooked and pour the melted butter over all and season with salt & pepper.

❋ Top with the cheese and serve immediately.

❋ At this point you may divide between serving bowls and top with your favorite sauce, or serve as a common dish topped with a sauce.

Brown sage butter is nothing more than a full stick of butter melted in a skillet with five or six leaves of sage and cooked until it begins to lightly turn brown and smells nutty. Chop up the sage leaves after cooking them in the butter and pour the brown butter and chopped leaves over the gnocchi. Top with the Parmesan if desired.
serves 4 generously

Note: A good shortcut is to purchase frozen gnocchi and add your own sauces. While not as light and tasty, there are some good brands in the grocery stores.

Vegetables

Provençal Tomatoes

For every French cookbook written there is a version of these tomatoes. We think our version would have pleased Axel and we are sure it will please you! Additionally, Max suggests you look at this dish as a way to use bits of leftovers in the refrigerator, as there is no hard and fast rule as to what should go onto the tomato top.

3 firm ripe round summer tomatoes
2 Tbsp. (30 ml) unsalted butter, softened
2 garlic cloves (2 tsp. [10 ml]) finely minced
2 tsp. (10 ml) minced chopped parsley
3 tsp. (15 ml) sugar
4 Tbsp. (56 ml) dried fine bread crumbs
1 Tbsp. (15 ml) olive oil
Salt and pepper

✤ Cut the tomatoes in half horizontally.

✤ Remove the top stem carefully but do not cut too deep into the tomato.

✤ Turn cut side down on paper towels and allow to drain for 10 minutes. Then very gently squeeze out the seeds and liquid pulp.

✤ Sprinkle the cut sides evenly with sugar but do not use more than ½ teaspoon (2.5 ml) on each tomato.

✤ Mix together the butter, garlic, and parsley and divide between the tomatoes, spreading evenly and thinly over the cut sides.

✤ Toss the bread crumbs in the olive oil and salt and pepper. Divide over the top of the tomatoes.

✤ Bake in a preheated 350°F (180°C) oven for 15 minutes. Serve as an accompaniment to any meat or fish main dish.

SERVES 6, ONE HALF EACH

Additional ideas are to drizzle a balsamic glaze over the top just after removing them from the oven. Also a sauté of finely chopped and cooked ground sausage mixed with the bread crumbs is delicious. Top with a bit of shredded Gruyère cheese in the bread crumbs. Take a light summer twist and add chopped fresh mint to the bread crumbs or go Italian with oregano or basil and parmesan cheese. If you were to have some left over vegetables like zucchini or spinach gratin you could chop it all finely and mix lightly with bread crumbs to bind and top the tomato with those leftovers. Chopped anchovies, tuna, and herring can all be mixed with the bread crumbs for a southern French twist. Maybe a touch of tapenade will inspire you to a different effect.

Le Fenouil à la Provençal

Fennel is a very French vegetable that is a staple in the winter. A light licorice flavor mixed with an earthiness overtone makes this inexpensive root vegetable a family favorite. Once you try it you too will be smitten!

4 large bulbs of fennel
4 Tbsp. (59 ml) olive oil
2 medium carrots
1 bouquet garni
1 cup (237 ml) fresh orange juice
Salt and pepper

❀ Remove the top ferns of the fennel and the stem root end.

❀ Slice the fennel in large ¼ inch round slices, using a mandolin if available.

❀ Do the same with the carrots.

❀ In a large heavy bottom skillet, heat the olive oil to medium high and sauté the fennel for 10 minutes.

❀ Season with salt and pepper and pour the orange juice over all.

❀ Add the bouquet garni and cover.

❀ Over medium low heat simmer for 35 to 40 minutes, until the fennel is tender to the fork.

❀ Remove the lid and raise the heat for 3 to 4 minutes to reduce the sauce. Serve with any meat dish or fish.

SERVES 4 TO 6

Fennel in Tomato and Garlic Sauce

4 large bulbs of fennel
4 firm ripe tomatoes
4 Tbsp. (59 ml) olive oil
1 large minced onion
5 garlic cloves chopped
1 cup (237 ml) chicken stock
Salt and pepper

❀ Remove the top ferns of the fennel and the stem root end.

❀ Slice the fennel in large ¼ inch (.6 cm) round slices, using a mandolin if available.

❀ Plunge the tomatoes into a pot of boiling water for 1 minute and transfer to a colander to cool. Cut an "X" in the top and pull off the skin. Cut into fourths and gently squeeze out the seeds.

❀ In a heavy bottom skillet heat the olive oil to medium high and sauté the fennel for 10 minutes.

❀ Add the tomatoes, onion and garlic. Sauté for 5 minutes with the fennel.

❀ Add the chicken stock. Cover and simmer for 40 minutes.

❀ Test for tenderness and if needed continue to simmer for 15 minutes longer.

❀ Remove the lid and taste and adjust the salt and pepper. Raise heat for 5 minutes to reduce the liquid.

SERVES 4 TO 6

Carrots in Vermouth

1 lb. (454 g) baby carrots cleaned and topped
2 Tbsp. (30 ml) butter
1 Tbsp. (15 ml) finely chopped fresh parsley
1/4 cup (59 ml) sugar OR honey
1/3 cup (79 ml) dry white vermouth OR dry white wine
Salt and pepper

❀ Place the carrots in a sauce pan of boiling water and blanch for 3 minutes until just barely tender. Drain.

❀ In a medium skillet melt the butter until frothy and add the carrots and sauté for 2 minutes.

❀ Add the parsley and the sugar and stir over medium heat until the sugar has dissolved.

❀ Add the vermouth and take care as it may flame, which is acceptable.

❀ Simmer over low heat until the liquid has reduced to a nice sauce-like consistency, about 3 minutes. Taste for seasoning and add salt and pepper lightly.

SERVES 4

Petit Pois (Baby Green Peas)

For a fresh, bright contrast on any main course plate, peas offer the solution and the flavor to please the palate.

3 cups (708 ml) fresh shelled or frozen baby peas
½ cup (118 ml) small diced bacon
⅓ cup (79 ml) finely diced onion
1 Tbsp. (15 ml) olive oil
Salt and pepper
1 Tbsp. (15 ml) butter

❀ In a heavy bottom skillet heat the olive oil to medium hot and sauté the diced bacon until just beginning to brown. Do not cook too crisp.

❀ Add the onion and sauté for 2 more minutes until the onion is translucent. In a sauce pan add ⅓ cup (79 ml) of water and a dash of salt.

❀ Bring to a boil and add the peas and bring back to a boil for 2 minutes.

❀ Drain completely, add the bacon and onion mixture and the butter and gently fold all together until the butter is melted. It is important that you do not overcook the peas or they lose flavor and turn grey green. Serve hot.

SERVES 4 GENEROUSLY

Font du Broc Winery, Les Arcs

Roasted Cauliflower

This is a very simple but delicious dish that can be roasting while you attend to other parts of your meal. You may also use this process with broccoli, or blend cauliflower and broccoli together for more taste and color.

1 medium head of fresh cauliflower
2 tsp. (10 ml) Herbs de Provence
2 Tbsp. (30 ml) olive oil
Sea Salt and pepper
1Tbsp. (15 ml) olive oil

❋ Wash and peel off bottom leaves of the cauliflower and remove the inner core of the head, leaving the head whole.

❋ Place it in an ovenproof casserole with just 2 tablespoons (30 ml) of water in the bottom.

❋ Drizzle the olive oil over the entire head of cauliflower and sprinkle with the Herbs de Provence.

❋ Add about 1 teaspoon (5 ml) ground black pepper and 2 teaspoons (10 ml) sea salt.

❋ Place in a preheated 350°F (180°C) oven and bake for 30 to 40 minutes until the top edges begin to turn golden brown and a skewer inserted into the center feels little or no resistance.

❋ Drizzle with 1 more tablespoon (15 ml) olive oil and serve immediately cut into portions.

SERVES 4 GENEROUSLY

Haricots Verts avec Almonds

1 lb (450 g) Fresh Thin Green beans
½ cup sliced almonds
½ cup (118 ml) butter
Salt and pepper

❋ Trim the stem ends of the beans.

❋ In a skillet, melt the butter and sauté the almonds for 3 minutes until well coated and starting to lightly brown.

❋ In a pot of salted boiling water plunge the beans and bring back to a boil. Boil for 4 minutes and drain well.

❋ Toss gently with the almonds and season with salt and pepper. Serve immediately.

SERVES 4 TO 6 AS A SIDE

Haricots Verts avec Almonds

Florentine Spinach

This is one of my favorite side dishes and once your family tastes it, will become one of theirs also. Fresh spinach in the market places in France usually comes in two or three sizes. In the States it is available in cello bags as well as in England and Australia. All will work after you remove the stems. Of course your cuisine jardin may be your best source!

6 cups (1420 ml) fresh spinach
½ cup (118 ml) minced onion
½ cup (118 ml) diced bacon
2 Tbsp. (30 ml) olive oil
½ tsp. (2.5 ml) ground nutmeg
2 large onions thinly sliced
2 Tbsp. (30 ml) olive oil
4 Tbsp. (59 ml) seasoned bread crumbs
½ cup (118 ml) shredded parmesan cheese
Salt and pepper

❋ Wash and roughly chop the spinach and set aside to drain very dry or wrap in paper towels and gently squeeze out all the moisture from washing.

❋ In a skillet heat the 2 tablespoons (30 ml) olive oil and sauté the bacon for 4 minutes.

❋ Add the onion and sauté for 2 minutes. In a heat-proof casserole or au gratin dish place the sliced onions evenly on the bottom and drizzle with the second 2 tablespoons (30 ml) of olive oil. Lightly salt and pepper.

❋ In the skillet fold together the spinach with the bacon mixture and lightly salt and pepper.

❋ Place evenly over the sliced onions. Blend together the bread crumbs and the parmesan cheese and sprinkle evenly over all. Place in a preheated 350°F (180°C) oven.

❋ Bake for 25 minutes until the bread crumbs lightly brown. Cut into individual servings and serve with a main meat or fish course.

SERVES 6

Zucchini Soufflé

All year round the French markets have various types of zucchini from little striped round balls to large, glistening green and yellow to the standard size garden variety. Any will work just fine in this recipe. You can make one large soufflé or individual ones in 6 oz. ramekins.

1 Tbsp. (15 ml) butter
¼ cup (59 ml) olive oil
1 yellow onion minced
2 garlic cloves minced
3 medium zucchini grated with
  skin on, squeezed dry
Salt and pepper
½ tsp. (2.5 ml) nutmeg
¼ tsp. (1.2 ml) cayenne pepper
6 eggs separated
8 oz. (1 cup) (237 ml) Gruyere or Swiss cheese
  grated
¼ cup (59 ml) minced parsley

Zucchini Souffle

❀ Preheat the oven to 350°F (180°C).

❀ Grease the ramekins or soufflé dish with the butter.

❀ Chop the zucchini into chunks and place in the food processor using the steel blade and pulse until the zucchini is finely grated. Place in a strainer and allow to drain for 30 minutes. Squeeze out any excess liquid.

❀ In a skillet heat the oil to medium high and sauté the onion and garlic for 4 to 5 minutes until translucent but not brown. Lower heat if necessary.

❀ Add the zucchini and sauté another 8 minutes over medium heat. Add the salt, pepper, nutmeg, and cayenne. Mix gently.

❀ Drain off any liquid that has occurred and set aside to cool or remove to a cool platter or bowl. You will need to press the mixture through a fine strainer to make it dry or the soufflé will not rise.

❀ With a mixer, beat the egg yolks until well blended then add the cheese with a dash of salt and pepper. To the cooled zucchini mixture add parsley and blend by hand with a wooden spoon.

❀ In a cool clean bowl add the egg whites and beat with clean beaters until stiff peaks form but not until dry. Add ⅓ of the egg whites to the cooled zucchini mixture and fold in gently. Add the remaining egg white mixture and again fold in gently until all is blended.

❀ Spoon into the ramekins and bake 30 minutes for individual ramekins or 50 minutes for a full soufflé dish, until golden on top and puffed. Serve immediately.

SERVES 6

Roasted Asparagus with Balsamic Lemon butter

2 lbs. (907 g) thin fresh asparagus, bottoms
  trimmed
3 Tbsp. (14 ml) soft butter
1 Tbsp. (5 ml) aged Balsamic vinegar
Juice of one lemon
Salt and pepper
Zest of one lemon

❀ Preheat oven to 350°F (180°C).

❀ Wash and trim the tough bottoms of the asparagus. Spread the soft butter in the bottom of a rectangular ovenproof dish. Place the asparagus on the butter, in a single layer, with tips all facing the same direction.

❀ Mix together the vinegar and the lemon juice and drizzle it over all the asparagus.

❀ Season with salt and pepper. Roast for 20 minutes in the preheated oven. Test for doneness but do not over bake. Asparagus should still have a bit of crispness to the bite.

❀ Remove to a heated serving platter and sprinkle with the zest. Serve immediately.

SERVES 4 TO 6

Sauté de Champignons

These earthy mushrooms are a delicious side to serve with lamb, beef or pork. Any mixture of fresh mushrooms will work fine, but always try to use three varieties for the best flavor and interest.

1 lb. (454 g) Baby Bella's
1 lb. (454 g) Chanterelles
½ lb. (227 g) Morel's
¼ cup (59 ml) olive oil
⅓ cup (79 ml) unsalted butter
4 roughly chopped garlic cloves
1½ tsp. (7 ml) Herbs de Provence
¼ cup (59 ml) dry white wine
¼ cup (59 ml) fresh chopped parsley
Salt and pepper

❧ Wipe mushrooms clean of any growing medium. Remove stems. Do not put into water.

❧ Cut any extra large mushrooms in half. If using dry Chanterelles and Morels, reconstitute them in hot water for 15-20 minutes. Drain well. Pat dry with towels.

❧ In a large sauté pan melt the butter and oil together until very hot but not browning.

❧ Add the mushrooms and sauté for 5 minutes.

❧ Add the garlic and white wine and continue to sauté for 5 minutes.

❧ Add the herbs and the parsley and blend well while continuing to sauté for 2 or 3 more minutes.

❧ Serve immediately in a heated serving dish.

SERVES 4 TO 6 GENEROUSLY AS A SIDE

Any leftovers can be chopped and folded into an omelet for breakfast. (Who am I kidding? There will be no leftovers!)

This is Axel's old sauté skillet from France.

A loose interpretation of General De Gaulle's famous declaration about cheese… "How can anyone govern a country that makes over 500 cheeses" …is known to many French food enthusiasts and Francophiles. Obviously he managed for a time. His observation was truly a statement on the many and delicious cheeses of that country, which most often are served as a course just before dessert. During my time in Les Arcs I was fortunate to be invited to numerous dinner parties where a cheese course was served. I had already become a bit addicted to this custom and now had the opportunity to discover many stellar cheeses from all over the country.

At La Terrasse Restaurant I discovered a cheese course that was the main course; Reblochon, a mild light yellow soft cheese made in little wooden cases and baked in the case until bubbly and lightly browned on top. By baking in the wooden box, a light woody flavor is imparted into the cheese. A tender crust forms, which is chewy and carries the toasty flavor, that is eaten on the little crostini served on the platter along with chunks of peeled and boiled potatoes and thick slabs of smoked bacon, all of which the diner dips into the soft, warm cheese. This cheese comes from the Savoy region that boarders Switzerland and Italy, north of Grenoble and is considered an Alpine cheese. Tres magnifique!

In the marketplace there are always a few cheese artisans selling fresh chèvre or fromage frais from their own farms and kitchens. These soft, mild goat cheeses have no rind and often are offered with a coating of cracked red or black peppercorns, herbs du Provençe, or fine ash (to encourage ripening). Sometimes I found

"banon" or rounds of cheese wrapped in chestnut leaves and tied in natural grass string. It is made from a variety of milks; goat, sheep or cow and the chestnut leaves impart a nutty, earthy flavor to the cheese. Served broken up on a salad it is a great addition to greens and presented on the chestnut leaves on a cheese service it holds its own just sitting on a toasted baguette slice.

Other cheeses found in the marketplace include semi-hard cheeses such as Cantal or Port-du-Sault, and the vendors provide small bites or shavings for the shopper to taste, each professing theirs is unique and, of course, the best in the region! Some of these cheeses are made by fifth and sixth generation families who have raised their goats (or sheep) on the same grazing land for hundreds of years, using the same method of production for as long.

Each region of France is known for specific types of cheeses, and the government grants a special designation to cheese makers known as the AOC. This means that the cheese is produced using specific methods unique to the region. The French name for this is "Appellation d' Origine Contrôlée" and allows the producer to affix a special stamp that indicates it is a traditional cheese approved for the AOC. Small local producers often do not have the designation, but that does not mean their cheese is of any less quality than that of the larger regional producers. One vendor in the local market in Les Arcs had a delicious Emmental cheese and only one or two other selections without the AOC. All were very tasty and reasonably priced.

One of my personal favorites is the Roquefort cheese from the Languedoc. A number of years ago I spent my annual journey to Southern France in the small village of St. Chinin in the Languedoc, and found an excellent Roquefort in the weekly market place. The town of Roquefort-sur-Soulzon is north of this village, but the cheese is famous all over France. Aged in limestone caves, the blue lines of flavor are nurtured with a mould that only grows in that climate.

A discussion of all 500-plus cheeses of Frances is a book unto itself and I am sure cheese experts will find this short commentary lacking much vital information about French cheeses. Axel does not dwell on cheese in his journal, yet it is included in numerous dishes. Over 100 years ago he may not have had as easy access to all the cheeses of France that are available today.

No matter where you live, the selection of cheese around the world has grown over the years and you should be able to present a lovely cheese board to family and friends after your meal, preceding the dessert course. Only three or four selections are necessary and often the cheese course with a nice wine, baguette and fresh fruit can be the end of the meal, prior to the coffee service. Be sure to allow the cheese to come to room temperature for best flavor. Presenting the whole block or round on a cheese platter, basket or board is the best method, allowing your guests to each cut their own choices. If you cut the cheese in advance it may form hard skins on each piece and not be as tasty or attractive. A set of three cheese knives is a good investment if you plan on serving this course often. And when choosing the cheeses to serve you may want to select from different categories', always including a familiar cheese such a Camembert or Brie and adding an unusual cheese such as Stilton, a wonderful English cheese and then a Danish cheese like Havarti to round out the selection.

"If I had a son who was ready to marry, I would tell him 'Beware of girls who don't like wine, truffles, CHEESE, or music'"
—Colette

Desserts

Desserts in France can range from fresh fruit with sorbet to stacked gateau (cakes) to fruit tarts and mousses to almond filled pastries and hundreds of other regional and traditional favorites. Creperies abound in France and the Creperie in Les Arcs offers a long list of sweet crepes. Many French cookbooks feature a Tarte Titan or poached pears

in wine or crème brûlée, so we have endeavored to offer some desserts that are not as well known, yet just as delicious, and traditional. Café Gourmand is another French dessert that is an assortment of mini desserts and a frothy coffee served on a pretty tray for just one person!

Peach Melba

The book would not be complete without including the famous Peach Melba recipe that Escoffier created for Dame Nellie Melba, a well know opera singer of his day. At the lovely Musee Escoffier de Art Culinaire in Villeneuve-Loubet, just near Nice, there are a number of photos of Miss Melba and copies of the recipe. If visiting southern France, a trip to this museum is well worth the time.

Poached Peaches

2 cups (473 ml) water
2 cups (473 ml) sugar
2 teaspoons (5 ml) vanilla extract
Half a cinnamon stick
3 whole cloves
3 firm ripe cling free peaches

Raspberry Sauce

1 cup (237 ml) fresh raspberries
¼ cup (59 ml) sugar
2 Tbsp. (30 ml) of Chambord liqueur
1 container best quality vanilla ice cream
Fresh mint leaves

Poached Peaches

❊ Combine all of the ingredients except the peaches in a saucepan. Bring to a gentle simmer, stirring to melt the sugar.

❊ Cut the peaches in half vertically, remove the pit. Gently clean out the pit area with a small spoon.

❊ Add the peach halves to the poaching liquid. Place a small plate on top of them to keep them submerged. Poach until tender. The time will vary depending on the ripeness of the peaches.

❊ To assure they are completely poached, insert a thin small knife and if there is no resistance the peaches are done poaching.

❊ Remove from the heat and allow to cool for 30 minutes.

❊ Place in the refrigerator and cool completely. This step may be done a day ahead of serving.

Raspberry Sauce

❊ Rinse and drain the raspberries and place them in a food processor. Puree them for 2 minutes.

❊ Place them in a small saucepan. Add the sugar. Bring to a simmer and cook for five minutes, stirring to avoid the sauce sticking or scorching.

❊ Add the Chambord and simmer briefly.

❊ Strain this sauce thru a fine strainer to remove the raspberry seeds. Allow the sauce to cool to room temperature.

❊ In attractive dessert dishes or large, broad champagne glasses, place a spoon full of the raspberry sauce and top with a rounded scoop of the vanilla ice cream.

❊ Place a poached peach slice on top of the ice cream and drizzle a bit more of the raspberry sauce over the top. Garnish with a fresh mint leaf if available. Serve immediately.

SERVES 6

Preparing for luncheon service at Le Logis du Guetteur.

Ile Flottante

FLOATING ISLANDS

My very first exposure to this traditional French dessert was in 1978 in New York City when I had the opportunity to study privately with Maurice Moore-Betty, chef and instructor. It was during the summer and just one other student was in the class, Helen Wasserman from Washington, D.C., chef and caterer. Since then I have experienced these wonderful little "islands" in various restaurants around the world, none better than what Max prepares at Le Logis du Guetteur. Easy to prepare and just three easy steps to assembly. Axel prepared them at many family dinners. Often they are prepared as one large meringue in the center of a large platter surrounded by the crème anglaise and spun with the caramel. Instructions to do this follow the more typical method.

The Islands
4 large egg whites
⅔ cup (158 ml) superfine sugar
½ tsp. (2.5 ml) vanilla extract
Pinch of salt
2 cups (500 ml) whole milk

✤ Prepare a non-stick skillet with the 2 cups of whole milk and bring to a low simmer. (You will poach the meringue in this milk and then use it for the crème anglaise.)

✤ In a clean, dry, and chilled metal bowl, place the egg whites and a very small pinch of salt.

✤ With clean, dry, and chilled beaters on a mixer, beat the whites until soft peaks form.

✤ Add the sugar and vanilla and continue to beat until stiff peaks form.

✤ Using two large tablespoons, form a round ball of the meringue and slide into the poaching milk.

✤ Poach for about 3 minutes, using the spoons to gently turn them to evenly poach on all sides.

✤ Lift with a slotted spoon to a platter.

Crème Anglaise
4 egg yolks
⅔ (158 ml) cup sugar
1 tsp. (5 ml) vanilla extract

✤ Beat the egg yolks until frothy and add the sugar and continue beating until the mixture is light and airy about 4 to 5 minutes.

✤ Add the warm milk from the poaching pan to the egg mixture and whisk until it begins to thicken. Do NOT allow to boil or it will separate and you will have sweet scrambled eggs!

✤ Pour into a spouted pitcher and cool completely.

Caramel
⅓ cup (79 ml) superfine sugar
1 Tbsp. (15 ml) water
¼ tsp. (59 ml) lemon juice
3 Tbsp. (44 ml) toasted sliced almonds

✤ In a small sauce pan place all the ingredients, except the almonds, and heat until it begins to turn a caramel color.

✤ Pour ⅓ cup (79ml) of the crème anglaise in the bottom of individual dessert plates.

✤ Place a meringue in the center of the crème anglaise. Sprinkle each meringue with some toasted sliced almonds.

✤ Using a tablespoon dip into the caramel and "spin" loops and drizzles of the caramel over the top of the meringue. Allow some to land on the crème anglaise. Your choice of fresh fruit for decoration will enhance the presentation. Serve immediately.

SERVES 4

Note: Leftover crème anglaise can be used with fruit desserts, chocolate or apple tarts, etc. Refrigerate for up to 5 days covered.

⊙ *To make just one large meringue, you may bake the meringue in a charlotte mold that has a piece of buttered parchment paper in the bottom and one on the top of the meringue and set in a Bain Marie containing boiling water in a 250°F (100°C) oven for about one hour.*

⊙ *To test for doneness, slip a thin paring knife into the middle and if it comes out clean the meringue is finished. If not, continue to bake for another 10 minutes before testing.*

⊙ *Remove from the oven and remove the top paper and invert onto a plate and take off the bottom parchment.*

⊙ *Cool and continue as if it were an individual meringue, using a large deep-sided serving platter to contain the crème anglaise.*

⊙ *Cut at the table and spoon the crème onto individual dessert plates.*

Tarte aux Pignons

PINE NUT TART

This traditional tarte is delicious served with either ice cream or even a swirl of crème anglaise on the plate bottom. It's not too sweet yet has an intriguing flavor with the honey and almond flour ingredients.

1 sweet pastry tart crust (page 135)
½ cup or 4 oz. (118 ml) almond powder
½ cup or 4 oz. (118 ml) superfine sugar
¼ cup or 2 oz. (59 ml) honey
½ cup or 4 oz. (118 ml) butter, softened
4 eggs
½ cup or 4 oz. (118 ml) pine nuts (pignon nuts)

❀ Preheat the oven to 350°F (180°C).

❀ Roll out the pastry and line a removable bottom 9 or 10 inch (23-25 cm) tart pan with the pastry. Crimp and cut the edges.

❀ With a mixer, mix the butter and the honey until well blended and creamy. Add the eggs one at a time beating until blended. Add the sugar and almond powder* and fold in gently but completely with a rubber spatula.

❀ Put mixture into the tart shell.

❀ Spread the nuts evenly over the top of the filling. Bake for 20 minutes or until the filling is set and the crust golden.

SERVES 6 TO 8

*In France almond powder is readily available. In the USA it can be difficult to find, so make your own by processing whole almonds in a food processor until they form a fine "flour" like texture. Take care not to over process or you will end up with almond butter!

Tarte au Citron

This is one of my favorite French desserts. Full of the lemon flavor, almost makes my lips pucker. It is light and refreshing any time of year and settles the tummy after a heavy meal or hits the spot after a light meal of salad and cheese. Serve with good strong coffee and if you can't decide between a citrus or chocolate dessert, fine decorative swirls of chocolate Ganache on the top will satisfy both desires.

1 portion of sweet pastry crust
4 eggs
1 cup (237 ml) superfine sugar
⅓ cup (70 ml) soft unsalted butter
5 Tbsp. (74 ml) heavy cream
Juice of 4 lemons
Fine zest of 3 lemons
Lemon zest strips for garnish

❋ Preheat oven to 375°F (190°C).

❋ Prepare the sweet pastry crust. Roll out the dough and line the removable bottom tart pan with the crust, pressing it into the edge crimps and cutting off any excess at the top edge. Line the bottom and up the sides of the crust with baking parchment paper and gently press into the bottom and sides of the pan. Place your baking beads or dried beans into the pan and bake for 12 minutes.

❋ Remove the beans or beads and parchment. Lower the oven temperature to 325°F (160°C). Place the tart pan on a cookie sheet tray. Bake for 5 more minutes to dry the crust bottom.

❋ Mix the butter and sugar together well by beating with a mixer for two or three minutes.

❋ Add the cream and blend well. Add the eggs, one at a time and blend well.

❋ Add the juice and the zest and blend well. Pour into the tart pan and place in the oven on the cookie sheet.

❋ Bake for 40 minutes or until the center is set and looks slightly bumpy. Cool completely before cutting or refrigerate 2 to 3 hours.

❋ Place the lemon zest strips in ice water to gently curl and drain on paper towels before garnishing the top of the cooled tart.

SERVES 6 TO 8

Note: You can reuse the dried beans for future crust baking. Store beans in a glass jar. Using a cookie sheet under the tart pan prevents the bottom from lifting up when placing the tart in or removing from the oven.

Orange Soufflé

Nothing in the desert department is more French than a good soufflé and an orange soufflé is the perfect ending to a lovely dinner.

6 8 oz. individual ramekins, buttered and sides
*   dusted with sugar to top*
3 cups (710 ml) whole milk
1 Tbsp. (15 ml) cornstarch
¾ cup (177 ml) sugar
7 egg yolks
2 Tbsp. (30 ml) Grand Marnier or orange liqueur
⅓ cup (79 ml) orange juice (juice of
*   approximately two fresh oranges)*
Fine zest of one orange
7 egg whites, chilled
3 Tbsp. (44 ml) superfine sugar

❋ Preheat oven to 400°F (200°C).

❋ In a small sauce pan, boil the orange juice until it is reduced to syrup and makes 4 tablespoons (59 ml) of concentrate syrup. Cool completely.

❋ In a double boiler with simmering water place the milk with the cornstarch dissolved in a bit of the milk beforehand. Stir well to blend and heat through.

❋ Add the beaten egg yolks and ¾ cup (177 ml) sugar. Whisk to combine well and keep over the simmering water, stirring constantly until mixture begins to thicken.

❋ Add the Grand Marnier and blend well.

❋ Add the orange syrup and zest and blend well. Cool 30 minutes.

❋ Whip the egg whites with the 3 tablespoons (44 ml) of sugar until peaks form and stand, but not too dry.

❋ Fold in a small portion of the whipped eggs to the orange milk mixture and then gently fold the egg mixture into the whipped egg whites until completely blended, taking care not to deflate the air of the whites any more than necessary to blend.

❋ Scoop mixture into the individual ramekins' and place on a cookie sheet.

❋ Run your thumb around the inside top edge of the ramekin, to create a little "ditch."

❋ Place in the preheated oven for 20 minutes until the soufflé s have risen and turned golden on top. If they jiggle, bake a bit longer.

❋ Serve immediately before they fall from the internal air cooling that makes them deflate.

❋ Garnish with powdered sugar or strips of the orange peel placed in ice water to curl a little and then drain on a paper towel. (Do this before you remove the soufflés from the oven so the strips are ready immediately.)

Note: To fold an ingredient into another is to use a flat rubber spatula or flat wooden paddle and gently pull the ingredients from the bottom of the bowl up and over the ingredients you are blending together and turning the bowl each time you make this motion until all is incorporated. Gentleness is of the essence.

Peche Dame Blance

This very simple dessert was a hit in the late 1800's and can be a hit today using purchased but good quality vanilla ice cream.

3 fresh firm, ripe peaches
1 fresh pineapple peeled and sliced into ½ inch
  rounds, core removed
½ cup (118 ml) Kirsch liqueur
1 qt. (960 ml) vanilla ice cream
½ cup (118 ml) whipped Chantilly cream

❀ Drop the peaches in a large pan of boiling water for 1 minute. Remove and slip off the skins, cut in half top to bottom and remove the pith.

❀ Soak the pineapple in the Kirsch for 10 minutes.

❀ Scoop the ice cream into dessert dishes (stemmed for a more elegant look) and place a peach half cut side up on the ice cream.

❀ Top with a slice of soaked pineapple and finish the top with a swirl of Chantilly.

❀ If there is any Kirsch remaining, drizzle a teaspoon of it over the top of the Chantilly. Garnish with a fresh mint leaf if available.

SERVES 6

Baba au Rum

In the Thursday market in Les Arcs, there is a man that sells Babas in five different sizes. There is a story that a duke of Lorraine created the first Babas out of kugelhopf, a firm bread with currants, of the north of France baked in a mold. He added some rum and declared a new dessert named after Ali Baba from the book *A Thousand and One Nights*. This is probably a myth but it makes good story to tell while serving this dessert. You will need special molds for this recipe, available in any gourmet equipment shop or department store housewares section. They come in different sizes and I recommend the individual portion size unless you wish to serve two or three very small ones in a crème anglaise or rum syrup.

¼ oz. of dry yeast or 8 grams if in a foil package
2 Tbsp. (30 ml) warm milk
1 cup (237 ml) of regular flour
1 tsp. (5 ml) of salt
2 Tbsp. (30 ml) superfine sugar
4 eggs beaten well
⅓ cup (79 ml) of small dried currants OR ⅓ cup
  (79ml) of finely chopped golden raisins
¼ cup (59 ml) dark rum
4 Tbsp. (59 ml) hot water
4 Tbsp. (59 ml) soft butter

Simple Rum Syrup
½ cup (118 ml) hot water
¾ cup (177 ml) dark rum
1½ cups (355ml) white sugar

✤ Bring the water and rum to a boil and blend in the sugar well and allow to simmer for 20 minutes until it very slightly begins to reduce and thicken. Cool and reserve for the Babas.

✤ Put the currants or raisins in the rum and water to soften. Set aside.

✤ Preheat the oven to 375°F (190°C).

✤ Place the warm milk in a warm bowl and add the yeast and allow to sit and dissolve for a few minutes.

✤ In a large room temperature bowl, (the bowls need to be warm to help maintain the action of the yeast; a cold bowl will kill the yeast) place the flour and in the center of the flour make a well and pour in the lightly stirred yeast mixture.

✤ Add the eggs on top of the yeast and begin to mix with your clean hands. (Alternatively this can be done in a stand mixer with a dough hook. Make sure the bowl is warm.)

✤ Mix the flour yeast mixture until it is smooth and slightly elastic, about 7 to 8 minutes.

✤ Pick up the dough and spank it like a baby's bottom to knockout the air. Put back into the bowl and put a warm damp tea towel over the top.

✤ Set it in a warm place out of drafts and allow to sit for about 1 hour until it has doubled in volume.

✤ If using real Baba molds, butter them well and place in the refrigerator to firm up the butter.

✤ Once the dough has risen, beat the 4 tablespoons (59 ml) of soft butter and work it into the dough kneading to form a soft smooth dough, about 4 or 5 minutes.

✤ Fill the molds about half full and tap down to completely fill in the mold. When all the molds are half full set them on a cookie sheet and cover with a damp warm towel for 20 to 25 minutes until they have risen to the top of the molds.

✤ Place in the preheated oven and bake until they begin to pull away from the sides of the molds, about 20 to 25 minutes, depending on the size of your molds.

✤ Remove and immediately unmold and allow to cool completely.

✤ The following day place the Babas in hot rum syrup and allow to soak up as much syrup as possible.

✤ Use a slotted spoon or fish turner to gently turn and remove them. They will get bigger in size as they soak up the syrup.

✤ Gently place on a platter or serving dish and cool.

✤ To serve, place on a warm dessert plate and drizzle the remaining hot rum syrup over each. Also a teaspoon of rum can be added to each at this time. Delicious served with Chantilly cream or crème anglaise.

SERVES 8 WITH TWO EACH

CAN BE FROZEN AND USED WITHIN ONE MONTH

304

✤ Baba
½ lb flour ¼ lb butter 3 onces sugar salt little milk and 5 whole eggs put a smale quantite from the ½ ble flour add to the one once of yeast Work the other with the rest of the flour and a handfull of currant.

Muffin Pate
once butter 8 ounce flour half gill milk tea spoon full Bokingpowder salt and little sugar melled Butter Bakingpowder sugar mark the whole vell together

Corn Moffines
3 tass of coffe + farine 2½ tass de smeulle 1 tass de sugar 3 cuilliere de Bakingpowder et du lai

Wheat Cake and Waffels
1 live de farine 2 aufs 2 once sucre 2 cuillere a café Bakingpowder et du lait, pour le waffers tenir la pate un peu plus dur (et une cuillere de beurre fondu) Buckwheat Cake
avec la farine de Buckwheat
Rice Cake
½ live farin de Rie et ½ lit farin le rest la men

129

Gateau Chocolat

This cake is also good for anyone who is gluten intolerant as there is no flour in the recipe. It is however, quite rich and small slices can be sufficient for almost anyone, served with fresh whipped cream or vanilla ice cream, or just dusted with dark cocoa.

6 oz. (170 g) of dark semi-sweet chocolate (70% if available)
¾ cup (177 ml) butter cut in pieces
1 cup (237 ml) + 2 Tbsp. (30 ml) superfine sugar
¾ cup (177 ml) dark cocoa (not the beverage mix)
4 large or 5 medium eggs well beaten
1½ tsp. (7.5 ml) vanilla extract

❊ Preheat the oven to 325°F (190°C). *

❊ Prepare a 10 inch (25 cm) cake pan with a round of baking parchment in the bottom that is buttered on both sides. Sprinkle the top side of the parchment with cocoa and shake out any that did not stick to the butter.

❊ In a glass or metal bowl placed over a pan of simmering water, (bottom not touching the water), place the butter and the chocolate and allow to melt completely, stirring occasionally.

❊ Remove from heat and stir in the sugar, cocoa, eggs and vanilla. Stir well and pour into the prepared pan.

❊ Set the cake pan in a larger pan of hot water that comes half way up the sides of the cake pan (Bain Marie). Bake 30 to 40 minutes.

❊ Cool 10 minutes and then turn out on a rack to cool completely.

❊ Prepare Ganache recipe if desired and spread over the top up to the edges.

❊ Slide off rack to serving platter.

❊ Garnish with whole almonds, chocolate curls, candied orange, or whatever fits the occasion.

Ganache

8 oz. (227 g) dark chocolate
⅓ cup (79 ml) heavy cream

❊ In double boiler, melt the chocolate with the cream and blend until smooth.

❊ Chill until slightly thickened and por over cake.

SERVES 8 TO 10

Baking

CÉRÉALES 1.65€
(200 gr / 8.25 kg)

LE BOISÉ 1,75€   CAMPAGNE
(400 gr / 4.37€ kg)   (200 gr / 5.50 kg)

$\mathcal{W}$here do "Desserts" leave off and Baking begin? In this section we offer our favorite Fougasse stuffed with savory goodies, our favorite pastry crusts, both savory and sweet, plus other essential recipes. The fine line between desserts and baking is often blurred, but in Provence it is all part of the gastronomic dance of eating.

The "Le Boisé" was my weekly ration of bread from the Boulanger while living in Les Arcs. Early in the morning it was still warm from the oven and welcomed me with its rich grain aroma. If I waited until 10 am, I was usually out of luck,

COMPLET 1.60€
(200 gr / 8€ kg)

10€   CAMPAGNE 1.40€
(400 gr / 3.40 kg)

until I learned to have one reserved. The desserts of the same establishment were alluring and hard to resist.

The recipe for the Pain du Potiron was good anytime and the aroma filled my French kitchen, reminding me of days long ago at my grandmother's farm kitchen in Pennsylvania. It is a people pleaser, as few people do not like pumpkin. There are many recipes that could go in this section, but for now these are part of the whole for this book. Enjoy!

Crème Anglise

Use this traditional sauce with fruit, cake, tarts and, of course, Ile Flottante. It keeps in the refrigerator for up to 5 days with plastic wrap placed directly on the top of the crème to avoid a skin from forming.

2 cups (473 ml) whole milk
6 egg yolks
¾ cup (180 ml) superfine sugar
2 tsp. (10 ml) vanilla extract OR 1 vanilla pod

✾ In a heavy bottom sauce pan over low heat, simmer the milk with the vanilla pod that has been split open, for 15 minutes.

✾ Remove the pan from the heat and allow to cool with the pod still in the milk. Strain the milk and discard the pod.

✾ In a bowl beat the egg yolks and the sugar with a whisk or mixer until light and lemon colored.

✾ Reheat the milk over low heat and slowly add half of it to the egg mixture, whisking constantly.

✾ Pour the egg mixture back into the pan with the remaining milk and very slowly simmer, whisking constantly, until the mixture begins to thicken. Do not boil or the mixture will curdle and be unusable.

✾ Once the mixture has thickened pour into a clean bowl and cover with plastic wrap placed directly on the top of the sauce. Refrigerate until ready to use. Bring back to room temperature before serving with your dessert.

MAKES APPROXIMATELY 2½ CUPS (591 ML)

Pate â Choux

This cream puff recipe is a standard in France, and has a number of applications. A pastry bag fitted with a large tip is required to pipe out the round mounds of the pastry for baking into golden little puffs. Filled with sweet cream anglaise, or a cheese filling as an appetizer, they are light and delicious.

2 cups (473 ml) water
¼ lb. (1 stick) (450 g) unsalted butter
2 cups (473 ml) sifted flour
½ tsp. (2.5 ml) salt
7 large eggs
1 Tbsp. (15 ml) sugar

✾ Bring the water to a boil with the butter and salt. Boil until the butter is fully melted.

✾ Remove from the heat and add the flour. Return to a medium heat and vigorously beat the mixture with a wooden spoon. The mixture will begin to pull away from the sides of the pan.

✾ Again remove from the heat and allow to cool for 8-10 minutes.

✾ Beat in the eggs one at a time until all are well incorporated and the dough begins to become shiny and very smooth.

✾ Beat in the sugar well and spoon into a pastry bag.

✾ Chill in the refrigerator for at least one hour before piping onto a baking sheet. Pipe 1½ inch (1.5 cm) rounds of dough for a regular crème puff and smaller for appetizers.

✾ Bake in a preheated 375°F (190°C) oven until golden brown and puffed, about 15 minutes.

MAKES APPROXIMATELY 30 REGULAR PUFFS

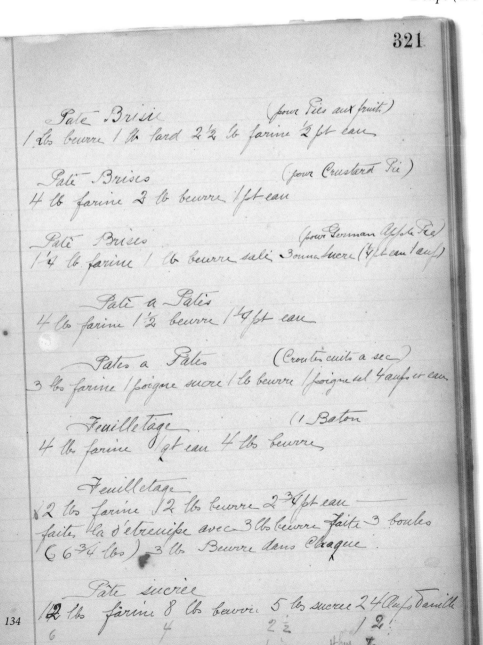

Sweet Pastry Crust

2½ cups (591 ml) all-purpose flour
¼ tsp. (1 ml) salt
¾ cup (180 ml) cold unsalted butter
¾ cup (180 ml) confectioners' sugar (powdered
 sugar)
2 eggs
1 Tbsp. (15 ml) ice water

❁ Sift all dry ingredients (flour and salt) together, in a food processor fitted with a steel blade.

❁ Cut the cold butter into small pieces and add to flour in the processor.

❁ Pulse on/off for 1 to 2 minutes until a coarse mixture forms like oatmeal consistency.

❁ Add the sugar and pulse 1 minute to blend.

❁ Beat the eggs well and, with the processor running slowly, pour into the mixture.

❁ Pulse 30 seconds. Add the water and pulse 30 more seconds.

❁ Turn out onto a floured surface and lightly knead a few times to make the pastry smooth.

❁ Divide the pastry into two pieces and wrap in plastic wrap and chill at least 1 hour or overnight for next day use.

❁ Roll out on a floured surface and place in pie or tart pan to bake.

MAKES 2 GENEROUS 9-INCH (23 CM) SHELLS

Savory Pastry Crust

2 cups (473 ml) regular white flour
7 Tbsp. (104 ml) chilled unsalted butter
2 medium eggs
2 tsp. (10 ml) salt
4 Tbsp. (59 ml) sour cream

❁ Place the flour and the chilled butter cut into pieces into a food processor.

❁ Pulse for 30-40 seconds until the mixture looks like cornmeal.

❁ With the motor running drop in the eggs one at a time until blended but do not over-process.

❁ Add the salt and pulse a few times.

❁ Drop in the sour cream and pulse a few times.

❁ Turn out the pastry onto waxed paper, form into a flat round ball and loosely wrap and chill for 30 minutes. It is very important you do not over work the pastry or handle it too much with your hands.

At the Patisserie in Les Arcs.

Pain du Potiron

PUMPKIN BREAD TEA SANDWICHES

In the market place in the fall and winter the merchants sell "cuts" of a very large pumpkin. These big, tan "potirons" have a wonderful, nutty flavor when roasted. Simply lay them in a roasting pan or on a cookie sheet with sides and add water to cover the bottom of the pan. Bake in preheated 350°F (177°C) oven until a thin paring knife inserted into the thickest part receives no resistance. Remove from the oven and allow to cool. Scrape the meat out of the shell and place in a strainer over a bowl and allow to drain for 2 hours. Push out any remaining moisture and place 2 cup portions in freezer bags. Freeze until ready to use in breads, pies, or galettes or for Soupe du Potiron. Or use immediately as needed.

3½ cups (828 ml) regular flour
2 cups (473 ml) dark brown
  sugar (soft sugar)
⅔ cup (160 ml) fine white sugar
2 cups (473 ml) pumpkin puree
1 cup (237 ml) Canola oil
⅔ cup (160 ml) coconut milk
2 tsp. (10 ml) baking soda
  (Bicarbonate)
1 tsp. (5 ml) salt
2 tsp. (5 ml) ground nutmeg
2 tsp. (5 ml) ground cinnamon
⅔ cup (160 ml) toasted coconut
Optional: 1 cup (237 ml) toasted
  chopped walnuts (Noix)

✤ Preheat oven to 350°F (177°C).

✤ Grease and flour 2 medium loaf pans. Place the baked pumpkin in a food processor and puree to smooth.

✤ In a large bowl combine all ingredients except the coconut and walnuts. Mix well until all is blended together.

✤ Fold in the coconut and walnuts. Pour into the baking pans. Bake 1 hour and 15 minutes, until a toothpick comes out clean when inserted in the very middle. Remove from oven and immediately cover very tightly with foil for 10 minutes.

✤ Remove the foil and turn out onto cooling racks and place foil loosely over the loaves until completely cool.

✤ Wrap tightly in plastic wrap until using. Refrigerate at least 2 hours for better results when slicing.

✤ Cut into ¼ inch (.5 cm) slices and cut slices into triangles. Spread with cream cheese spread for tea sandwiches.

Cream Cheese Spread
1 package Philadelphia regular cream cheese,
  softened
2 Tbsp. (30 ml) powdered sugar
1 tsp. ground cinnamon
½ tsp. grated nutmeg
1 Tbsp. heavy cream or crème fraiche

✤ Mix all together and spread on the pumpkin bread triangles.

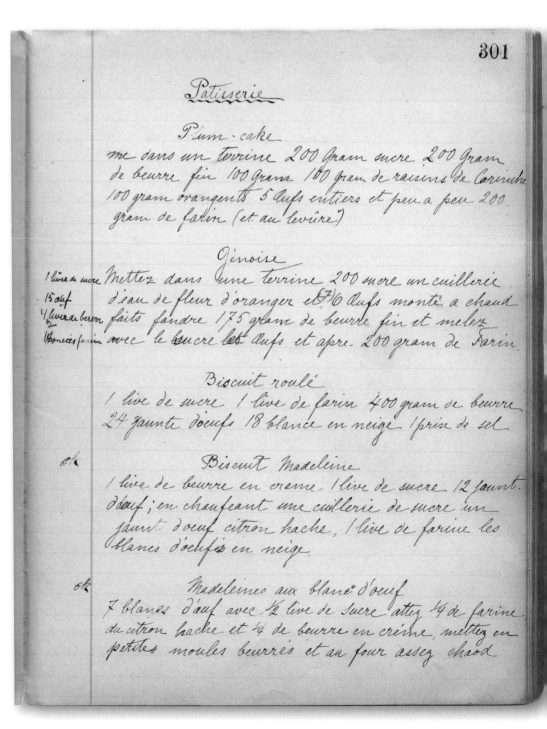

Across the walkway from Karen's house.

Fougasse

This is a very typical Provençal bread found at most all boulangeries. Fillings vary according to the baker and the regions. My sister Susan refers to this as a "French Calzone" and it is even tastier than its Italian counterpart. Additionally you may use this dough for just nice, unfilled loaves of bread, by allowing it to rise a second time before forming loaves. Brush with olive oil and some sea salt or herbs before placing in the oven. This recipe is much easier than its length may indicate and once you have made this remarkably easy dough you will find many ways to create new recipes of your own.

Dough

2½ cups (591 ml) white all-purpose flour
2 pkgs. (½ oz./14 grams) dry yeast (may be quick rise)
1¼ cups (296 ml) warm water
3 Tbsp. (44 ml) extra virgin olive oil
½ tsp. (2 ml) salt

Filling

¾ cups (180 ml) sun dried tomatoes (in oil) roughly chopped
1 2 oz. (56 g) anchovies in oil
1 cup (237 ml) rough chopped artichoke hearts
1 cup (237 ml) rough chopped pitted kalamata olives
½ cup (118 ml) rough chopped garlic cloves
½ cup (118 ml) shredded Emmental cheese or shredded Parmesan Cheese
Sea salt
Olive oil

❋ Preheat Oven to 375°F (200°C)

❋ Sift the flour and salt together in a large bowl.

❋ In a separate small bowl or measuring cup with the warm water, sprinkle the yeast over the water. (Water must be just warm, not hot or the yeast will die.) Allow to sit for a minute or two and then stir to dissolve any lumps.

❋ Add the yeast mixture to the flour and add the olive oil. Mix well with a wooden spoon.

❋ On a floured work surface turn out the dough and knead the dough by pulling, folding, and punching it down, turning and repeating the process for about 5 minutes.

❋ Oil the inside of the bowl and return the dough to the bowl in a ball, turning to coat well with the oil.

❋ Cover with a damp towel and set in a draft free warm place for 1 hour or until doubled in size.

❋ Turn out on a lightly floured surface and punch down. Cut the dough into two or three pieces depending on how many loaves you wish to make.

❋ Roll out the dough into rectangular shapes approximately 6 inches by 12 inches (15-30 cm).

❋ Spread the anchovies, tomatoes, olives and artichokes on one long side of the dough, leaving a 1 inch (2.5 cm) margin to seal.

❋ Fold the dough over the filling and pinch together on the filling side.

❋ Place on a baking sheet with the seam on the bottom and tuck the ends under.

❋ Using a very sharp knife or razor blade slice diagonal slits in the top to expose the filling. Stretch the slits open a bit with your fingers.

❋ Brush the loaves with olive oil and sprinkle with sea salt and the cheese.

❋ Bake in the preheated oven for 30 minutes or until golden brown.

❋ Brush with olive oil again upon removing from the oven.

MAKES THREE LOAVES

Fougasse for Christmas

In France the Christmas Eve dinner includes a traditional service of 13 desserts, including little bits of nuts, nougat, citrus, and other delicacies in tiny portions.

❋ The Fougasse is adapted for this occasion by adding ½ cup (118 ml) sugar to the flour mixture, the zest of one big orange and 2 tsp. (10 ml) of orange water and one egg yolk.

❋ Reduce the water by ¼ cup (59 ml) to allow for the orange water and egg yolk.

❋ Roll out ½ inch (1.5 cm) thick as directed, after a second rising, and make many slashes in the dough to look a bit like a Christmas tree.

❋ Bake as directed above for 20 minutes, sprinkle with superfine sugar immediately after removing from the oven.

MAKES THREE LOAVES

Sauces & Dressings

Throughout the book we have referred to other pages for additional recipes, most of which are found here in the Sauces and Dressings section. While the Escoffier bible is full of various sauces, he always maintained a light hand in applying the same. It is a misconception that excellent French cooking is swimming in sauces and creams.

As for dressings for salads, you will find three very good basic recipes. The second is a family favorite of mine that I have used for years, both at home and in my restaurant. A true French dressing is not orange as we have been lead to believe in America!

The only other important sauce is found on the page with Soupe du Poisson: a Rouille for fish soup or for dipping fresh veggies.

Sauces & Dressings

Hollandaise Sauce

5 egg yolks
2 Tbsp. (30 ml) fresh lemon juice
1½ cup (355 ml) hot melted butter, clarified
1 tsp. (5 ml) cayenne pepper
1 tsp. (5 ml) salt

✤ Place egg yolks in a blender, reserving the whites for another use (they can be frozen and used within a month).

✤ Add the lemon juice and blend on medium speed for 1 minute.

✤ Bring the butter to a boil in a heat-proof glass pitcher in the microwave or in a pan on the stove.

✤ Skim off the milk fats that float to the top and discard (this is clarifying the butter).

✤ With the blender running on medium speed slowly drizzle the hot butter in thru the top opening in the lid of the blender.

✤ Add the cayenne pepper and the salt and blend 1 more minute. The mixture should be thick and creamy. Will keep up to 3 days in the refrigerator, covered. Bring to room temperature to serve.

Note: Putting the sauce in a squeeze bottle with a medium point opening allows for a more attractive presentation when serving.

Béchamel Sauce

6 Tbsp. (89 ml) unsalted butter
1 large shallot finely diced
¾ cup (177 ml) flour
3 cups (710 ml) whole milk, hot
1 cup (237 ml) veal or chicken stock, hot
½ tsp. (2.5 ml) ground nutmeg

✤ In a heavy bottom saucepan over medium heat melt the butter to just foaming in the pan.

✤ Add the shallot and sauté until transparent but not brown. Do not allow the butter to brown.

✤ Lower the heat and add the flour and stir constantly, making a roux*. Continue stirring for about 3 or 4 minutes but do not brown the roux.

✤ Turn off the heat and slowly whisk in the milk.

✤ Add the stock and continue to whisk. You want the sauce to be very smooth after whisking each addition.

✤ Using a medium low heat return the pan to the burner and gently simmer for about 10 minutes. Add the nutmeg during this time.

✤ Adding a bouquet garni or a sprig of thyme and one of rosemary during the last simmering is traditional in French cooking.

✤ Using a fine mesh strainer, pour the sauce through the strainer into another sauce pan or into a bowl to reserve until serving.

✤ To set aside for a time, cover the sauce with plastic wrap sitting directly on top of the sauce to prevent a "crust" from forming.

*Roux is a French term for blending butter and flour to make a thickener. It is important that the roux be cooked enough to cook off the raw flour taste.

Mornay Sauce

A Mornay sauce is just a Béchamel Sauce with Gruyere cheese whisked in at the end and melted into the smooth sauce.

To the above Béchamel recipe simply add ¾ cup (177 ml) grated Gruyere cheese and whisk over a low heat for about 4 to 5 minutes, until well incorporated and smooth.

Three French Dressings for Salads

#1

> 1 Tbsp. (15 ml) Dijon mustard
> 2 Tbsp. (30 ml) red wine vinegar
> 1 cup (250 ml) extra virgin olive oil
> Salt and pepper to taste

✤ In a deep bowl whisk together the mustard and the red wine vinegar.

✤ Slowly drizzle in the olive oil while whisking continually. (Placing the bowl on a wet kitchen towel in the corner of the sink makes this much easier to control.)

✤ After the mixture has emulsified, add the salt and pepper. Store in a glass jar or use immediately to dress greens. Store for up to 1 week in refrigerator.

#2

> ¼ cup (59 ml) Balsamic vinegar
> 1 cup (237 ml) Extra Virgin olive oil
> ¼ cup (59 ml) honey
> 1 tsp. (5 ml) salt
> ½ lemon with rind, end cut off

✤ Place all ingredients in a blender and process for 3 minutes.

✤ Taste for seasoning and store in a glass jar or use immediately. Store for up to 1 week in the refrigerator.

#3

> 2 anchovies either tinned or jarred
> 1 cup (237 ml) extra virgin olive oil
> 1 Tbsp. (15 ml) lemon juice
> 1 medium garlic clove
> 1 Tbsp. (15 ml) balsamic vinegar
> Salt and pepper to taste

✤ Place all ingredients in blender and process for 3 to 4 minutes until slightly thickened and smooth.

✤ Taste for seasoning and store in a glass jar or use immediately. Store for up to 1 week in the refrigerator.

Remoulade Sauce

> 2 Tbsp. (30 ml) capers, drained well
> 1 medium shallot peeled and cut in half
> 4 medium cornichons or small dill pickles cut in half

1902 Dinner Menu

> 1 Tbsp. (15 ml) of fresh chopped chives
> 1 egg
> 1 Tbsp. (15 ml) Dijon mustard
> 1 tsp. (5 ml) salt
> 1 tsp. (5 ml) ground pepper
> 4 Tbsp. (59 ml) white vinegar
> 8 Tbsp. (118 ml) olive oil

✤ Place the capers, shallot, pickles, chives, egg, mustard, salt, pepper, and vinegar in a blender and process until well blended and as smooth as possible.

✤ Slowly add the olive oil a tablespoon (15 ml) at a time, until all is well blended.

✤ It will not be completely smooth but should be well incorporated and as smooth as possible. Adjust for taste if necessary.

143

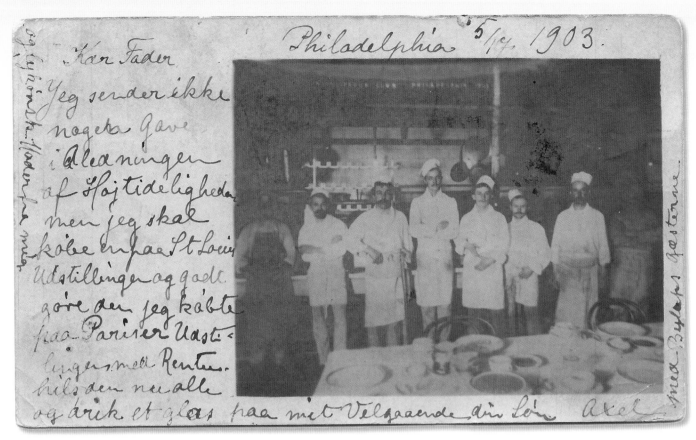

Axel with other chefs in Philadelphia, 1903.

Old French Brown Sauce

⅓ cup (79 ml) unsalted butter
⅓ cup (79 ml) flour
¼ cup (59 ml) tomato paste
¼ cup (59 ml) finely diced mushrooms
3 cups (710 ml) reduced beef stock (from 6 cups
  [1420 ml])
2 tsp. (10 ml) salt
1 tsp. (5 ml) pepper

❋ In a heavy bottom sauce pan over medium heat melt the butter until foamy.

❋ Add the flour stirring to combine well and eliminate any lumps.

❋ Add the tomato paste and the diced mushrooms and stir over medium heat for 2 minutes.

❋ Slowly whisk in the beef stock that you have previously reduced by half, keeping the mixture over medium heat and whisking for 5 to 6 minutes until smooth and thickened and somewhat slightly reduced.

❋ Add the salt and pepper.

❋ Strain thru a fine mesh strainer and store in a glass jar. Float a dab of butter on the top to prevent a skin forming. Can be stored in the refrigerator for 10 days, tightly covered.

This sauce can be added to the simple cream sauce or used as a brown sauce foundation diluted with a bit of hot water.

Mayonnaise

4 egg yolks
1 tsp. (5 ml) white wine vinegar
1 tsp. (5 ml) fresh lemon juice
1½ cups (355 ml) canola oil, peanut oil, or rape
  seed oil
1 tsp. (5 ml) salt
1 tsp. (5 ml) white pepper

❋ Using a blender, process the egg yolks and the vinegar and the lemon juice until well blended.

❋ Remove the top of the lid center and very slowly drizzle the oil in while the blender is running on medium speed.

❋ Taste for seasoning and adjust if necessary. Store in a glass jar for up to 1 week in refrigerator.

Additions to this basic mayonnaise recipe could include anchovies, lemon or lime juice and/or zest, balsamic vinegar in place of the wine vinegar, smoked salmon, finely diced sautéed shallots, herbs, Dijon mustard, capers or cayenne pepper. Design your own flavored mayonnaise using a gentle hand with any additions!

Simple Cream Sauce

4 Tbsp. (59 ml) butter
3 Tbsp. (44 ml) flour
1 ½ cups (355 ml) whole milk heated to room
  temperature
1 tsp. salt (5 ml)
½ tsp. (2.5 ml) white pepper
1Tbsp. (15 ml) butter

❋ In a heavy bottom sauce pan over medium heat, melt the butter until foamy and add the flour, stirring to create a roux.

❋ Slowly add the heated milk, whisking continually until sauce thickens.

❋ Add the salt and pepper and lower the heat and continue to whisk 3 to 4 more minutes.

❋ Add the last tablespoon (15 ml) of butter and whisk for another minute. If there are any lumps, strain through a fine mesh strainer.

Note: This sauce can have any number of flavorings added such as nutmeg, cayenne, or beef or chicken base to accommodate the dish to which the sauce is being added.

Brown Sauce

3 Tbsp. (44 ml) unsalted butter
3 Tbsp. (44 ml) flour
1½ cups (355 ml) beef stock reduced from 3 cups
  (710 ml) of stock
1 tsp. (5 ml) salt
1 tsp. (5 ml) ground pepper
1 Tbsp. (15 ml) butter
1 Tbsp. (15 ml) Madeira Wine or Sherry
  (optional)

❋ In a heavy bottom sauce pan over medium heat melt the butter until foamy.

❋ Add the flour and stir to blend well until the mixture becomes medium brown but taking care not to get it too dark or burnt.

❋ Whisk in the reduced stock slowly as the sauce thickens.

❋ Add the salt and pepper and continue to whisk.

❋ Add the 1 tablespoon (15 ml) butter and whisk 1 minute.

❋ Add the Madeira or Sherry and whisk for 1 minute.

❋ Strain thru a fine mesh strainer if necessary. Always taste for seasoning and adjust as needed.

Béarnaise

This traditional sauce is delicious on fish or steak or even a poultry sauce. Using fresh tarragon, if possible, is by far the most tasty, but dried will certainly suffice. I am offering this sauce in a modern fashion to facilitate the busy home cook. A traditional method is using a double boiler and whisking in the hot butter to the egg yolks and shallot mixture in a slow steady stream. An alternative method as one does not always have access to a blender!

3 Tbsp. (44 ml) dry white wine
3 Tbsp. (44 ml) white wine vinegar OR tarragon vinegar
1 Tbsp. (15 ml) lemon juice
1 Tbsp. (15 ml) chopped fresh tarragon OR 2 tsp. (10 ml) dried tarragon
2 Tbsp. (30 ml) chopped shallots OR white onion
1 stick/8 oz./½ cup (118 ml) of unsalted butter
4 egg yolks
½ tsp. (2.5 ml) cayenne pepper
Fine sea salt and fresh ground pepper to taste

❀ In a medium sized skillet over high heat, combine the wine, vinegar, lemon juice tarragon, shallots, and cayenne. Bring to a roaring boil and continue to boil until only 1 Tbsp. (15 ml) of liquid remains.

❀ Allow to cool off the burner for 10 minutes.

❀ Melt the butter in the microwave until hot and completely liquid.

❀ In a blender, place the egg yolks, and a dash of salt and pepper. Pulse to puree.

❀ Remove the top opening and slowly drizzle the hot butter into the mixture with the blender running.

❀ Turn off the blender and add the herbs and blend on high speed for only 30 seconds.

❀ Remove from blender with thin rubber spatula. The mixture will be very thick. Serve immediately or refrigerate, covered with plastic wrap on the top of the sauce to prevent a skin from forming.

Roux

A roux is a thickener for numerous dishes. Depending of the application you may want to cook the roux to just a very light golden tone or to a very dark brown tone. Darker roux is used in Creole dishes such as gumbo or to thicken a daube or soup. A light roux is normally used to thicken sauces and creams.

½ cup butter (118 ml)
¾ cup flour (177 ml)

✤ Melt the butter in a small skillet until foamy.

✤ Add the flour and blend well until a paste forms and pulls away from the sides of the pan.

✤ Continue to stir for 3 to 4 minutes to cook off the raw flour taste.

✤ Add some of the juice or stock from what you are trying to thicken to the pan and incorporate.

✤ Blend the skillet contents into the product being thickened a bit at a time to avoid lumps.

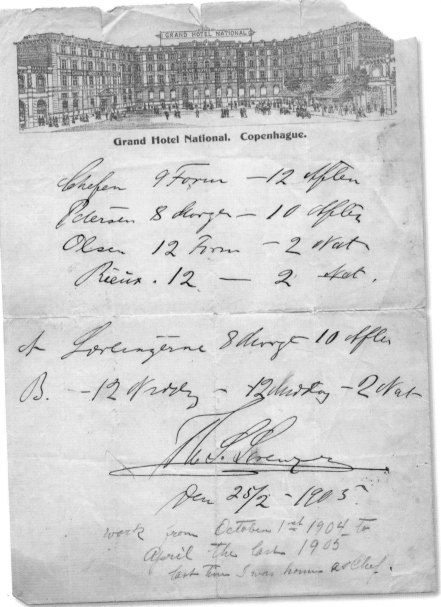

Grand Hotel National. Copenhague.

Aioli

10–12 peeled garlic cloves, minced
1 tsp. (5 ml) salt
2 large egg yolks
1 tsp. (5 ml) of white mustard (Moutarde de Dijon)
1½-2 cups (355-473 ml) fine olive oil
White pepper to taste (about 1 tsp. or 5 ml)

✤ In a blender put the egg yolks, a little mustard, and add by drops the olive oil. When the mixture gets thick add the minced garlic, salt and pepper. You then have what they call in Provence an "Aioli".

✤ Put into a glass jar and refrigerate until needed. Will keep for one week in the refrigerator. It must not be too cool otherwise your Aioli could separate.

Melba Cocktail Sauce

2 Tbsp. (30 ml) horseradish
½ cup (118 ml) tomato catsup
¼ cup (59 ml) Melba sauce or strained blackberry jelly

✤ Blend all together and chill until needed.

Herbed Mayonnaise

There is nothing easier in the world than to make a mayonnaise and it is so much tastier.

1 cup (237 ml) mayonnaise (not salad dressing)
1 Tbsp. (15 ml) Dijon mustard (Moutarde de Dijon)
2 tsp. (10 ml) Herbs de Provence
1 garlic clove well mashed

✤ Mix all the ingredients well in a blender or food processor.

✤ Place in a glass bowl and chill until needed.

A reference from the Grand Hotel National in Copenhague.

Les Arcs sur Argens

This wonderful old village that welcomed me with open arms during the winter and spring of 2012-13 holds a very long history of intrigue and fascination. A Medieval fortress that began in the 900s and changed hands over the centuries, huddles on a rocky outcropping high above the current village along the Réal River, with its double walls offering just four gates of entry. Its maze of cobbled stone streets wind up steeply to the chateau, offering views over the valley below as far as the eye can see.

Les Arcs at dawn

The Medieval Village or Parage , as the current residents refer to it, boasts the "Saracen Tower," which is home to the Le Logis du Guetteur, restaurant and hotel, called this due to the tower being a place from which to guard against the Saracen invasions in the 12th century. The Parage is a double walled fortress that maintains much of its history in the renovations that have occurred over the years. A wonderful little museum tells the story of the history of the village and sits at the top of the third entrance.

Plan du Parage

① LE DONJON
Seul vestige du château construit
par Giraud II de Villeneuve au XIII° siècle.

② LA TOUR DE L'HORLOGE
Tour de flanquement carrée incluse
dans les remparts en 1358.
La tourelle de tuf supporte un
superbe campanile (1662),
chef-d'œuvre à six faces.

③ PLACE PAUL SIMON
On y voit l'ancien édifice
de « l'Espital des Pàvres
de Jésus-Christ », hospice
et lieu d'accueil
des déshérités.

④ CHAPELLE SAINT-PIERRE DU PARAGE
Ancienne paroisse Notre-Dame, mentionnée
pour la 1ère fois dans une charte de 1050.
Reconstruction fin XII°, début XIII° siècles,
avec modifications au XVI°.
Rénovation en 1960.

**⑤ L'ÉGLISE PAROISSIALE
SAINT-JEAN-BAPTISTE**
Cet édifice est dans la lignée
des églises provençales du XVIII° siècle
par le classicisme de l'ornementation.
Beaux décors dont le « Retable de
la Vierge » (voir ci-contre)
du peintre niçois Louis Bréa (1501).

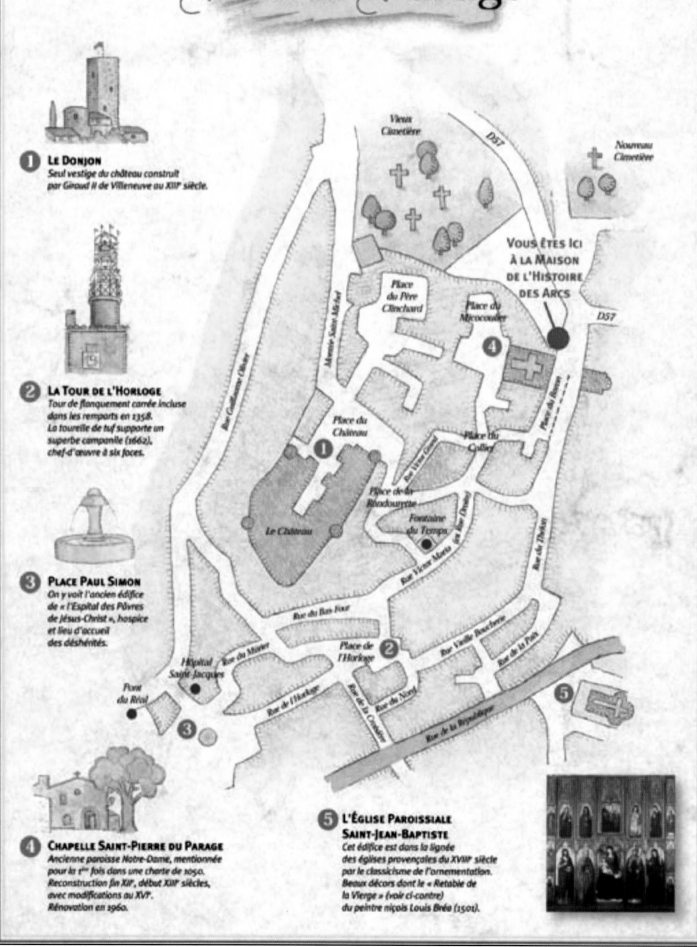

Sainte Roseline had a big influence on the village and today the Chapel St. Roseline, where she lies in state, the Convent and Winery just outside of town, reflect her life story while sitting guard over beautiful vineyards.

The commercial and residential parts of the city are of fair size. Shops along the Blvd. Gambetta offer various services and products, as well as the Café de la Tour. The Creperie and La Terrasse restaurants sit over on the newly renovated Place St. Michael. The beautiful Hotel de Ville, located at the Place de General de Gaulle, was refurbished in 2001 and is quite attractive as is the large patio and seating area in front. Further up the boulevard is a charming fountain not far from the Boules court.

Because of the Réal River, many mills were a big part of Les Arcs history as well as the large silk spinning mill; today a luxury B&B. These mills are just shells of their former buildings with the exception of one, Moulin du Haut that has been converted to a residence. Just down the street from there is the Le Petit Moulin, an early olive oil mill established in 1755. It is now a private residence.

For olive oil from the area the Thelon Moulin is located at the "back" of the Parage on Rue du Thélon. In the late fall and through the winter trucks pull up daily to unload the harvested olives to be pressed into olive oil. On Thursdays in the marché on the Rue Gambetta, this mill sells their wares in various sizes and even flavored oils.

Hotel de Ville

The big Church in the village, Eglise St. Jean Baptiste/ St. Sebastien, offers a panoramic model of the old village. For just one euro this village comes to life and light with music; located at the back of the beautiful church. Additionally there is a 19 panel polyptyque that was painted in 1501 and the artist is supposedly Louis Brea. It is in need of restoration but some panels still reflect the vibrant colors and beauty of earlier times.

Situated along the N7, Les Arcs is conveniently located near Draguignan, Le Muy, La Motte, and the famous Abbey Thoronet. Hiking trails abound and the sea is only a 30 minute drive south.

When one looks at the map of France, it is clearly a country flowing with rivers from every direction. The Rhone and the Saône join in Lyon and become the Rhone flowing down to the sea, forming a distinct border between Provence and the Languedoc. In Provence there is the Durance that also joins the Rhone, at Avignon. A tributary of the Durance is the Verdon River, which actually forms the Gorge du Verdon, the Grand Canyon of France. Farther southeast is the Argens River, creating the Argens valley at the very edge of the Maures Massif. Bordering the village of Les Arcs sur Argens on the south is the Argens River, into which flows le Réal that flows through the main part of Les Arcs from the north.

The Var river comes out of the Maritime Alps and flows southeast into the Mediterranean between Nice and Saint-Laurent-du-Var. Once upon a time it was actually part of the department of the Var, but over years the boundaries changed and it was no longer in its own department.

All these rivers and their small tributaries assist greatly in the irrigation of orchards, vineyards and gardening. The produce that comes from the Provence area is abundant and varied to the extent that Provence has been referred to as the "Market Basket of France." Fruit trees provide numerous types of fruit including the delicious cherries of Provence. The regional dish of ratatouille is just one example of the use of local vegetables that has withstood the test of time. Just a visit to the local weekly markets will attest to the wide selection of fresh vegetables and the home cook, as well as the cafés and restaurants, stock their kitchens from what is seasonally available in the market.

Numerous eateries are sprinkled throughout Les Arcs, offering many types of cuisine. In the square Place Paul Simon is the Créperie du Parage, not far from La Terrasse and the Boulangerie Pâtisserie Pezzulli. Just down the side street is the Oriental Restaurant, with delicious soups and platters. Further down is Café de la Tour, also featured in the salads section and La Boutique à Pizza. Continuing down the Boulevard Gambette is Brasserie des Sports, serving good comfort food for lunch. Across the Boulevard is Le Cabanon, featured in the salads section and further is Fleur de Sel, a quaint bistro offering a daily Plat du Jour and delicious Pizza. The Maison des Vin Côtes du Provence is located at the far end of town on the N7, with hundreds of regional wines to taste and select. In the same location upstairs is La Vigne a Table, an elegant white cloth dining experience. On the route de Sainte Roseline is a Michelin Stared restaurant, Le Relais des Moines. Also along the N7 towards Le Muy is the famous and very popular La Pinéde Pizzeria and Brasserie. And of course my favorite is Le Logis du Guetteur at the top of the Parage in the old château.

Les Arcs Mayor, Alain Parlanti, has worked tirelessly to restore much of the lower village after the devastating

Christine at Parage du Creperie
Crepes Chevre

Celine at La Terrasse
Chocolate Lava Cake

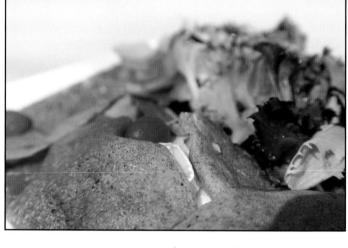

Crepes Jambon et oeufs

flood in 2010. He and the city fathers are forward thinking and look constantly to bring the village to total restoration, attracting industry, commerce and tourism.

In the surrounding area Les Arcs enjoys the bounty of the vineyards with many wineries. Le Cellier des Archers is the local cooperative offering very nice selections. Château La Font du Broc and Château Sainte Roseline are on the old road to La Motte and one of my favorites is a small boutique winery Domaine Valette on the route towards Draguignan. There is also Château Saint Pierre Route de Taradeau and Château Maïme on the N7.

Check with the tourist office (lesarcstourisme@ dracenie.com) for special events and points of interest when visiting this part of La Dracénie, located in the center of the village at Place du Général de Gaulle.

Les Arcs Mayor Alain Parlanti

Right: One of the four original entrances to the Parage.

St. Sebastien Church

AUGUSTE ESCOFFIER

SCHOOL OF CULINARY ARTS

Our Mission

Auguste Escoffier School of Culinary Arts empowers students to achieve their potential in the culinary and pastry arts through small class sizes and individual, modernized instruction in the techniques developed by the King of Chefs, Auguste Escoffier. Students are trained to understand where their food comes from and to develop respect for local resources and sustainable practices. Graduates enter the workforce with a balance of practical skills, humility and dependability.

The Auguste Escoffier Schools of Culinary Arts offer professional culinary arts programs based on the methods, principles and systems of Auguste Escoffier, the international culinary icon and the source of modern cooking. Students have the opportunity to learn history and context directly from the Escoffier family, as well as from expert chef instructors.

The Schools' Culinary Arts and Pastry Arts certificate programs offer rigorous industry skills training, as well as, grounding in the standards of professionalism and excellence sought by employers. Campuses are located in Austin, Texas and Boulder, Colorado.

In May of 2012, The Auguste Escoffier Schools of Culinary Arts, www.escoffier.edu, in Austin, Texas and Boulder, Colorado, announced the launch of a "Farm-to-Table®" experience at its Austin campus and a new "Sustainable and Ethical Cooking" course at both campuses.

Already a staple in Boulder, Austin's "Farm To Table®" experience provides students with the opportunity

to work side-by-side with local farmers and artisans. The hands-on experience provides students with information to aid them with distinguishing and recognizing alternative sources of food supplies while allowing opportunities to apply the techniques and methods learned in foundational and international courses of the Culinary Arts Program. In addition to working with local farmers and artisans, students will be able to utilize the school's new Urban Agricultural Center this fall.

The "Sustainable and Ethical Cooking" course being offered at both schools explores where food comes from, how chefs can benefit from this knowledge and the application of basic cooking techniques in the preparation of unique and alternative foods. Artisan techniques and production are introduced and students will compare and contrast local, sustainable versus conventional products.

"We are dedicated to providing our students with valuable and relevant curriculum that will further enhance seasonal and sustainable cooking methods associated with the Master Chef, Auguste Escoffier," said Paul Ryan, President of the Auguste Escoffier Schools of Culinary Arts.

For more information, visit www.escoffier.edu, call 866-552-2433 in Austin, or 877-249-0305 in Boulder, or follow us on facebook at www.facebook.com/escoffierschool.

Acknowledgments

By Karen Blumensaadt-Stoeckley

It goes without saying that this book would never have become a reality without the dedication of Max Callegari. Long winter hours were spent at my kitchen table pouring over the many recipes that just suggested ingredients and no measurements or procedures. I will always be indebted to Max for his steadfast diligence in reading and translating the old handwriting of my grandfather. Max's talents in the culinary arts brought a wonderful dimension to the book that is a true reflection of the food of France and, in particular, Provence. Additionally, Max created many of the recipes for the photography at his restaurant in Les Arcs, along with his superb staff that assisted in many ways with table settings, glasses of wine and fresh pressed linens. To share equal billing with Max as author is an honor and privilege.

A huge thank you goes to Curt Dennison, photographer extraordinaire! I have had the good fortune to work with Curt on food photography for many years and a lifetime friendship has formed between us. He traveled to Les Arcs with his chef son Stephen Dennison, and they quickly were embraced by the folks of the village while Curt worked his magic with the camera. Stephen assisted in Max's kitchen as well as assisted Curt in the photography process.

Curt fell in love with Provence, especially the people and the food, and his work in this book reflect this love. He truly made the recipes come alive in each shot. I will always savor the time we shared together in Les Arcs and always be extremely grateful for his support, encouragement and willingness to travel half way around the world to make my dream come true.

Another granddaughter of Axel's who contributed significantly to this book is my sister, Susan Blumensaadt Smith. Susan traveled to Les Arcs in November of the winter 2012 and consulted with me on the progress of the book. Additionally, she proofed the book completely several times, catching many of my typos and errors, helping to make the book very understandable to the reader.

Susan is an accomplished cook in her own right as well as a museum archivist, with degrees from University of Toledo, Indiana University and Wright State University. She has written and edited numerous articles and columns on history, cooking and gardening during her career. A master gardner,

her love of gardening not only manifests itself through her delightful flower gardens but in her abundant vegetable gardens where she endeavors to raise numerous heritage vegetables for her kitchen creations. For Susan's contribution and for the time it gave us together I am very grateful.

A great grandson of Axel's, my son Denton Mitcham, is to be thanked profusely for his interest and time he devoted to coming to Les Arcs to visit and encourage. Additionally, he came home to Missouri to assist me with much of the technical aspect of the book layout and design. The many hours he spent by scanning the old book to be just right for publication took patience and expertise. His enthusiasm for the book and for the final product was contagious and drew his cousin Kristine Blumensaadt Korver into the internet conversations for title considerations and design. Kristine offered the final selection for the title as she felt the original book was the legacy to us from

had arrived for me to leave the daily hustle and details of life and concentrate on getting the book translated and written.

Last, but certainly not least, I want to thank my publisher Doug Sikes, designer Frene Melton, and the entire staff at Acclaim Press for their time and devotion to bringing the book to the cooks of the world. Doug's vision of what the book would become was inspiring and his gentle patience with each step was truly a gift. The dependability and honest business ethics of Doug and the staff speak volumes of their dedication to this project. Thank you all.

Axel. I fully concur. Both of these great grand children of Axel's, along with my sister Susan, will keep his legacy alive for many generations to come.

For many of my friends who participated in meals of "photo food" and their honest and proper evaluation of the dishes, I am very grateful. Many of these same friends were strong supporters of my sabbatical to Les Arcs for the purpose of writing this book, and it was their love, support, letters and e-mails that bolstered me up during my winter/spring away.

Also, many of these people are my friends living in Les Arcs and the area and from St. Johns the Evangelist in San Raphael. To Tony and Jacqui, Jim and Pauline, Marie Claire, Alexandria and Andrew, Kim and Terry, Tina and Christian, Sylvia and Yves, Christina and Christophe, Sebastian and Celine, Inge Birget and Richard, Sheila and Melvin, Pat and John, Joost and Peter, Sven and Bjorg, June and Osbian, Sophie and all the ladies of the WWV, many, many thanks for your friendship and support.

To Michel Escoffier I shall always be very appreciative of his support for the book and his encouragement to carry on in the tradition of his great grandfather Auguste Escoffier. His generous offer to write the forward of this book attests to his commitment to see the Escoffier legacy continued to new and up coming generations of home cooks and professional chefs.

And to my husband, John Stoeckley, who held down the fort back home for six months, I thank him for encouraging me to make this book a reality. He knew the book was a lifelong dream and that the time

The Authors

Restaurant owner, executive chef, and culinary writer, most of Karen's adult career has been devoted to creating good food to feed family and friends as well as professionally feeding guests demanding only the best on their plates. Cooking, teaching and writing are her passions.

Her former restaurant in Louisiana, Missouri was located in the historic downtown area just a block from the Mississippi River. Located in four continuous buildings that were restored to their 1850's style, the property housed a Bistro and Fine Dining Restaurant, serving continental cuisine, a Dining Garden, Winery and Bakery along with eleven B&B Inn rooms. Good food, good service, and award winning wine was the keystone of her restaurant. The Winery, B&B Inn and the Bakery are still in operation.

Previous culinary experience includes a number of years in the 1970's as the Culinary Consultant to Le Creuset and Cousances, the wonderfully heavy vitreous enameled cast iron French cookware. That position afforded her the opportunity to teach cooking from Bloomingdale's Main Course in New York City to Macy's basement in San Francisco, as well as studying cooking in France, Italy, and the USA.

A summer spent with Maurice Moore-Betty in his NYC school was another opportunity that molded her culinary abilities. A brief stint in New Orleans gave Karen a peak into Cajun cooking and three years living in the Orient allowed her to study Japanese, Thai, and Chinese cuisine.

Karen and her husband, artist John Stoeckley, have traveled to Provence for fifteen spring/summers, where Karen has enjoyed the opportunity of cooking in her own kitchen with the abundance of produce from the local marketplace, as well as visit and work briefly in the kitchens of many successful chefs'.

Karen's balcony in Les Arcs.

A native of San Raphael, co author Max Callegari is a professionally trained chef from the Lycée de Lorgues and the Nice Hotel School, Nice, France. He trained and worked in restaurants in France, Italy and England, honing his culinary skills to take over the family business in 1980.

Max's father was a successful chef for many years, owning the renown Le Logis du Guetteur in Les Arcs sur Argens, at the top of this medieval village in the Parage. Having been raised in the restaurant and hospitality business, Max discovered the love of cooking at the elbow of his father. Today Max is not only the Executive Chef of the restaurant but a daily part of the kitchen team, creating exquisite dishes that reflect classic influences with modern flair.

Involved in the Tourism Authority of the Var, Max served as President of Logis de France in 2001 and later went on to be President of Les Maîtres Restautateurs Varois. In 2003 he received the Silver Medal from the Tourism Industry of France.

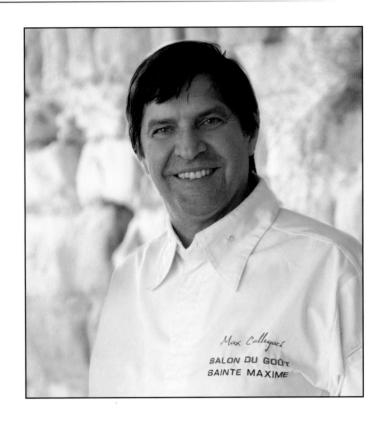

The Photographer

Curt Dennison

Curt Dennison began his career in art the moment that he was dismissed from kindergarten for coloring outside of the lines.

Curt is a 1982 graduate of Southern Illinois University at Edwardsville with a Bachelor of Fine Arts, majoring in painting and printmaking. He lives in Washington, Missouri USA with his wife and is a member of the Washington Rotary Club.

Curt has created photographs professionally since 1982 and has owned a free-lance commercial photography business since 1994. He photographs people, products, places, food, and agriculture for corporate, advertising, and industrial clients worldwide.

Index

Recipes

Le Creuset Products available at the following sites:
All William Sonoma Stores, www.williamsonoma.com
www.lecreuset.com
Sur La Table Stores

NOUVEAUX PRIX de VENTE

Denrées	Quantité par personne et mensuellement	Prix de Vente
Alcool à Brûler	2 litres par famille	2.50 le litre
Bougies	0k.250 d°	2.25 le paq.
Beurre	0k.250	de table 6f.90 le K°. / de cuisine 6f. "
Café	0k.500	6.40 le K°.
Chicorée	0k.250	3.20 d°
Chocolat	0k.500	5.00 d°
Choucroûte	1 kilog	0.70 d°
Crème de riz ou farine de riz	0k.250	crème 0f.70 le paquet 250 g / farine
Confitures	0k.250	2.50 le K°
Fromage	0k.500	4.00
Fécule	0k.250	1.60
Harengs	0k.500	2.0
Huile	½ litre	2.4
Légumes secs	1 kilog	lenti... / haut...
Lessive à Cristaux	d°	
Oeufs	Suivant disponible	
Pétrole (Suivant la carte qui va être mise en circulation)	2 litres par ménage	
Pâtes assorties	1 kilog	
	0k.500	
Sardine	1 boîte	1.2
Sel	0k.500	0.2
Saindoux / Végétaline	1 kilog	saindoux / végé
Savon	0k.400	1.
Sucre luxe		1.
Semoule	0k.500	2.
Tapioca 1 paqu...	0k.250	0.
	½ litre	0.8
	5 litres	1.8

WWII Ration poster from the kitchen of Corey Amaro, publisher of "Tongue in Cheek Brocante."